Digital Humanities and Libraries and Archives in Religious Studies

Introductions to
Digital Humanities – Religion

Edited by
Claire Clivaz, Charles M. Ess, Gregory Price Grieve,
Kristian Petersen and Sally Promey

Volume 5

Digital Humanities and Libraries and Archives in Religious Studies

—

An Introduction

Edited by Clifford B. Anderson

DE GRUYTER

ISBN 978-3-11-053432-0
e-ISBN (PDF) 978-3-11-053653-9
e-ISBN (EPUB) 978-3-11-053437-5
DOI https://doi.org/10.1515/9783110536539

This work is licensed under the Creative Commons Attribution-NonCommercial-NoDerivatives 4.0 International License. For details go to http://creativecommons.org/licenses/by-nc-nd/4.0/.

Library of Congress Control Number: 2021948487

Bibliographic information published by the Deutsche Nationalbibliothek
The Deutsche Nationalbibliothek lists this publication in the Deutsche Nationalbibliografie; detailed bibliographic data are available on the Internet at http://dnb.dnb.de.

© 2022 with the authors, editing © 2022 Clifford B. Anderson, published by Walter de Gruyter GmbH, Berlin/Boston
The book is published with open access at www.degruyter.com.

Cover image: Social network visualization. With friendly permission of Martin Grandjean.
Printing and binding: CPI books GmbH, Leck

www.degruyter.com

Table of Contents

List of Contributors —— VII

Acknowledgements —— IX

Clifford B. Anderson
Introduction —— 1

I Methodological Approaches

Michał Choiński and Jan Rybicki
Puritan Preachers in the Hands of Statisticians: The Stylometric Study of Colonial Religious Writings —— 13

Matthew Handelman
A Messianic Theory of Digital Knowledge: On Positivism and Visualizing Rosenzweig's Archive —— 31

Jeri E. Wieringa
Mining Eschatology in Seventh-day Adventist Periodicals —— 57

II The Database as Locus of Digital Humanities

Tracy Miller
Digital Humanities and the Interdisciplinary Database: Confronting the Complexity of Chinese Religious Architecture in the Academic Marketplace —— 79

Christine Schwartz
Using XQuery and XSLT to Build an Aggregation of Metadata Records for Religious Texts and Non-Print Items —— 95

III Digital Humanities Pedagogy

Richard Manly Adams, Jr.
Defining Digital Pedagogy in Theological Libraries —— 111

Clifford B. Anderson and Gayathri Narasimham
An Introduction to the Beauty and Joy of Computing for Theological Librarians —— 123

IV Collaboration and Beyond

Experimental Humanities Lab at the Iliff School of Theology
Library as Interface for Digital Humanities —— 147

Index —— 165

List of Contributors

Richard (Bo) Manly Adams, Jr., Director of Pitts Theology Library and Margaret A. Pitts Assistant Professor in the Practice of Theological Bibliography, Candler School of Theology, Emory University (Atlanta, Georgia, United States)

Clifford B. Anderson, Associate University Librarian for Research and Digital Strategy and Professor of Religious Studies, Vanderbilt University (Nashville, Tennessee, United States)

Michał Choiński, Associate Professor, Institute of English Studies, Jagiellonian University (Kraków, Poland)

Experimental Humanities Lab, Ira J. Taylor Library, Iliff School of Theology (Denver, Colorado, United States)

Matthew Handelman, Associate Professor of German and a member of the Core Faculty in the Digital Humanities, Michigan State University (East Lansing, Michigan, United States)

Tracy Miller, Associate Professor, History of Art and Architecture; Associate Professor, Asian Studies; Affiliated Faculty of the Graduate Department of Religion, Vanderbilt University (Nashville, Tennessee, United States)

Gayathri Narasimham, Research Assistant Professor, Computer Science Department, School of Engineering, Vanderbilt University (Nashville, Tennessee, United States)

Jan Rybicki, Associate Professor of English Studies, Institute of English Studies, Jagiellonian University (Kraków, Poland)

Christine Schwartz, Systems and Electronic Resources Librarian, Princeton Theological Seminary (Princeton, New Jersey, United States)

Jeri E. Wieringa, Assistant Professor in the Department of Religious Studies, The University of Alabama (Tuscaloosa, Alabama, United States)

Acknowledgements

I would like to thank Dr. Alissa Jones Nelson, then Acquisitions Editor in Religious Studies for De Gruyter, for the initial invitation to edit a volume in the *Introductions to Digital Humanities—Religion* series. Thanks also to the series editors, Dr. Claire Clivaz, Dr. Charles M. Ess, Dr. Gregory Price Grieve, Dr. Kristian Petersen, and Dr. Sally Promey, for including this work among the other excellent volumes. I also extend my thanks to Dr. Eva Frantz, Project Editor for Jewish and Islamic Studies at De Gruyter, for providing guidance during the beginning stages of this project and inviting me for coffee at the lovely De Gruyter headquarters in Berlin. I am equally grateful for Dr. Sophie Wagenhofer, Senior Acquisitions Editor, and Katrin Mittmann, Project Editor for Religion at De Gruyter, for seeing the project through to publication.

The availability of this volume in open access comes by way of financial sponsorship from Atla and the Divinity School Library of the Vanderbilt University Libraries. In particular, I would like to thank Brenda Bailey-Hainer, Executive Director at Atla, and Christine Fruin, Scholarly Communication and Digital Projects Manager at Atla, as well as the members of the Scholarly Communications Committee at Atla, for their support of this publication. I would also like to express my appreciation to Dr. Bill Hook, former Director of the Divinity School Library and Deputy University Librarian, and to Dr. Valerie Hotchkiss, former University Librarian and Professor of English, for their championing of this volume in particular and of open access generally at Vanderbilt University.

I am thankful for the digital humanities community at Vanderbilt University as well as for the members of Vanderbilt's Computational Thinking and Learning Initiative. This volume would never have come about without the encouragement and generosity of colleagues in the libraries and on the faculty of Vanderbilt University.

My wife, Dr. Rosanna Anderson, who is both a Presbyterian pastor and a professional proofreader, read through the early drafts and provided essential help in the preparation of the manuscript. My son, Theodore, put off lots of games and activities until, as he said, "Your book is done." Thanks to you both, I am happy to report it's now finished, so let's go out and play!

Clifford B. Anderson

Introduction

The title of this volume locates its contributions at the intersection of three broad communities of research and practice: the digital humanities, religious studies and theology, and library and information science. The members of these communities are active, diverse, and, at times, beset by internal tensions and contradictory tendencies. The essays in this collection all fall under the rubric of digital humanities but the volume does not aspire to map the territory. How would it be possible to identify their intersections as peripheries of activity and interests shift, let alone chart the zones of overlap? The chapters represent soundings, determining the depths and returning with proposals for future explorations.

What links these chapters together is shared commitment, from different positions in the academy, to advancing our understanding of religion and theology through the lenses of the digital humanities. But, along with commitment to the digital humanities, this volume also speaks to a shared ethos of collaboration across academic disciplines and hierarchies. While it has become commonplace to praise interdisciplinary scholarship, fewer acknowledge the professional costs or discuss the potential for reshaping institutional hierarchies. By adding librarians to the equation, addressing these topics becomes unavoidable. Whereas the other volumes in this series raise questions of digital humanities methodology or situate digital humanities within the study of particular religious traditions, what makes this volume distinctive is its emphasis on digital humanities emerging from generative partnerships between faculty and information professionals. In some cases, the collaborations take place tacitly, as information professionals prepare the digital sources that researchers then analyze and theorize about. In most cases, the collaborations take place explicitly, as projects grow in scale and sophistication beyond the scope of individual investigators and become shared initiatives. In special cases, as with the final essay in this volume (and with apologies to Marshall McLuhan), the partnership *is* the project.

That said, the contemporary call to interdisciplinarity in scholarship tacitly acknowledges an underlying truth about the academy. Namely, the academy tends to reward what Isaiah Berlin referred to as "hedgehogs," that is, those scholars who "relate everything to a single central vision, one system less or more coherent or articulate, in terms of which they understand, think, and feel–a single, universal, organizing principle in terms of which alone all that

---

OpenAccess. © 2021 Clifford B. Anderson, published by De Gruyter. This work is licensed under the Creative Commons Attribution-NonCommercial-NoDerivatives 4.0 International License.
https://doi.org/10.1515/9783110536539-002

they are and say has significance."¹ Hedgehogs find the academy a favorable environment because it rewards the compounding of their expertise over time. While their interests may wander or wobble, the centrality of their vision and the depth of their knowledge keep them from falling down rabbit holes. Would it be better to call them scholarly weeble wobbles? For practitioners of the digital humanities, the situation is radically different. The field of digital humanities, while celebrated and fêted as an interdisciplinary success story, has scarcely existed long enough for hedgehogs to take over. There are, of course, old hands whose experience stretches back to the years when the field was dubbed humanities computing and who know, for example, the markup of the Text Encoding Initiative like the proverbial back of the hand. But this project stretches back to the 1980s and, if you include SGML, back to the 1960s. The heritage of the TEI is thus no older than our millennial or GenX colleagues. Compare that to the generations of scholars who have published about Augustine, Al-Farabi, or Maimonides.

The scholars who venture into this morphing region are by nature adventurers, disdaining the blazed lines of ascent in the academy to chart new paths. To be fair, some abandon those paths of necessity because the old byways prove no longer passable, worn down by economic circumstances and administrative ill use and neglect. While the link between "alt-academic" career paths and the digital humanities may not be intrinsic, hacking new routes through the academy becomes more reasonable when barricades prevent access to the well-trodden career routes. Like all pilgrim travelers, faculty, librarians, and other "alt-acs" find companionship along the way, forging bonds as they surmount challenges and overcome obstacles to their progress.

The vocation of librarianship has long appealed to the foxes of the academy. Librarians who work in digital scholarship may find themselves discussing data management plans with historians, crafting data models for financial documents with accounting faculty, and prioritizing software enhancements for online liturgical calendars, all on the same day. The opportunity to range widely across scholarly fields proves simultaneously exhilarating and exhausting, especially at smaller institutions where so-called "miracle workers," to use the tongue-in-cheek term coined by Leigh Bonds and Alex Gil, are expected to serve, as Christina Boyles et al. write, as "scholars, tech support, administrators, project consultants, and more."² This antipattern frequently emerges at seminaries

---

[1] Isaiah Berlin and Michael Ignatieff, *The Hedgehog and the Fox: An Essay on Tolstoy's View of History*, ed. Henry Hardy, 2nd edition (Princeton: Princeton University Press, 2013), 1.

[2] Christina Boyles et al., "Precarious Labor and the Digital Humanities," *American Quarterly* 70, no. 3 (2018): 694, doi:10.1353/aq.2018.0054.

and other schools of theology, where two or three members of the library staff bear responsibility for everything from cataloging books to teaching information literacy courses. In such cases, jettisoning the effort to keep up with every new technique and tool becomes the only antidote to burnout. As Adams, Narasimham, and I argue in our chapters, embracing a more grounded, less tool-driven pedagogy in the digital humanities serves the long-term interests of students and faculty better anyway.

The chapters in this volume also underscore that projects in digital humanities range in scale and ambition. Librarians generally set out with at least an intuitive understanding of the significance of the digital humanities for the future of scholarship, having grappled since the 1950s and 1960s with the conversion of abstracts, indexes, and catalogs into machine readable formats while also recognizing how costly it is to make the collections they curate computationally tractable. The development of the Theological Commons, which Christine Schwartz describes in her contribution, originally involved a five member team of librarians and library staff members at Princeton Theological Seminary and built on the labor of several dozen more institutions to digitize their holdings in partnership with the Internet Archive.[3] For faculty just setting out in the field, the costs of digital humanities projects emerge slowly as their projects grow: a prototype database needs to be converted into something more robust, source control systems must be implemented, cloud services have to be coordinated, optical character recognition has to be corrected and markup applied, etc. By starting off in partnership, faculty and librarians have a better chance of anticipating and routing around these surprises, which may otherwise stymy progress.

Methodological Approaches

The difficulty with defining the digital humanities stems in part from the lack of shared methodologies. While digital humanists rely on computational methods in some form or another, the diversity of those techniques makes "computation" or "the digital" too broad to serve as a differentiator for the field. In the first section of this volume, three distinct approaches to the analysis of religious documents are featured, highlighting the potential and limitations of stylometry, network analysis, and topic modeling.

---

[3] Clifford B. Anderson, "Building a Theological Commons," in *American Theological Library Association Summary of Proceedings*, 66 (2012): 96–100.

In "Puritan Preachers in the Hands of Statisticians: The Stylometric Study of Colonial Religious Writings," Michał Choiński and Jan Rybicki of Jagiellonian University describe the complementarity of computational stylometry and the close reading of texts. Stylometry applies statistics to literary (as well as other) "texts" to analyze markers of style, seeking for the small "tells" in patterns of usage that distinguish genres and authors while also helping to demarcate, to cluster, and to periodize texts within oeuvres. As they indicate, stylometry represents an example of a technology that emerged prior to the advent of digital computers, but which used to take years of painstaking labor to carry out; nowadays, scholars may readily install open source packages for R and Python to carry out stylometric analysis. What remains challenging, of course, is how to apply and interpret the results to advance understanding of the texts.

In a series of studies in miniature, Choiński and Rybicki demonstrate how stylometric methods shed light on the affinities of Puritan preachers during the eighteenth-century Great Awakening in New England while also raising questions and ambiguities. The clusters in the network diagrams demand interpretation. Why, for instance, does the style of certain treatises by Jonathan Edwards (1703–1758) resemble his sermons more than his other doctrinal writings? Choiński and Rybicki's close reading of these texts provides some clarification of this surprising association. But challenging the status quo of Edwards (and, by extension, Puritan) scholarship is, in fact, the main purpose of their stylometric investigations. For scholars of religious studies and theology, these kinds of provocations may help to unsettle their familiarity with timeworn texts, prompting them to formulate novel arguments, if only on behalf of old convictions.

In a related vein, Matthew Handelman illustrates how surfacing the latent networks in scholarly archives challenges critical consensus. In "A Messianic Theory of Digital Knowledge: On Positivism and Visualizing Rosenzweig's Archive," Handelman, Associate Professor of German at Michigan State University, counters the charge that the digital humanities represent the return of positivism under a new guise. Taking as an example the archives of the Jewish philosopher Franz Rosenzweig (1886–1929), Handelman asks what the visualization of his extant correspondence reveals and also what it elides. The Rosenzweig archive is nowhere found in its totality, but is rather distributed across institutions in Germany and the United States with related materials in archives in Israel and elsewhere. As Handelman expands his network to include metadata from more of these collections, a persistent gap remains between the representation and reality of Rosenzweig's network. The "messianic archive" that exhaustively maps his social relationships always transcends the available data, however conscientiously assembled from the sources. While such network visualization can bring hidden figures to light (such as, in Rosenzweig's case, the significance of the Swiss-German poet, Margarete Susman, to his network of acquaintances), we must avoid becoming "seduced," Handelman cautions, by the promise of a complete and unified archive to come. This kind of metaphysical hope only reinforces a positivism that the digital humanities, at its ethically best, disowns and renounces.

Jeri E. Wieringa applies a different set of techniques to bring latent information to the surface in "Mining Eschatology in Seventh-day Adventist Periodicals." Wieringa, Assistant Professor of Religious Studies at the University of Alabama, was formerly the Digital Publishing Production Lead at the George Mason University Libraries. Having worked both as a library staff member and as faculty, she understands how digital librarianship supports (and, at times, fails to take account of) digital humanities scholarship.

Wieringa explores how textual analysis of denominational periodicals provides insight into the diachronic religious development of the communities of faith that wrote and published them. She applies a form of unsupervised machine learning called topic modeling to identify clusters of associated articles. Like the other contributors in this section, Wieringa observes that algorithmically-generated topics provide clues about shifting patterns of discourse over time, but are not self-interpreting. Scholars must not only draw narratives from data, but also interrogate the data themselves. Like Handelman, she notes the distance between the archival data available to scholars and the vanishing point of the ideal archive.

Here Wieringa returns to the collaborative conditions of labor and production that make possible the textual analysis of archival collections. How have the initial priorities for digitization affected the accessibility of relevant data? How have denominational politics shaped the availability of sources? If the page images were converted to textual format with optical character recognition, what is the rate of error? As information professionals seek to make more sources available to scholars of religion for analysis, they should develop closer partnerships to address such questions (and others) as they arise. While cost is always an inhibiting factor in digitization, slowing down the rate of production to create, clean, and curate datasets to make them more readily tractable for textual analysis would benefit not only individual researchers but the cause of digital humanities in religious studies as a whole.

The Database as Locus of Digital Humanities

The next two essays address the database as source and expression of scholarly knowledge. In the history of both librarianship and digital humanities, the database has played an ambiguous role. Librarians are wont to refer to the user interface of a system as "the database," using the term as a synecdoche for the complex platform of operating system, data retrieval systems, backend server technologies, and frontend web frameworks that compose contemporary information systems. This synecdoche may already have outlived its rhetorical usefulness in general information literacy, but it fails altogether in the digital humanities.

Tracy Miller, Associate Professor in the History of Art Department at Vanderbilt University, describes the process of creating the *Architectura Sinica* database in "Digital Humanities and the Interdisciplinary Database: Confronting the Complexity of Chinese Religious Architecture in the Academic Marketplace." She recounts the history of the project, which stretches back decades to her initial field research in China, where she captured images of architectural elements on slide film and kept notes in a bespoke word processor. As technologies evolved, Miller had to make decisions about how her project should evolve. How and where should she store her data and how ought she create interfaces for scholars? Miller's participation in the university libraries' Semantic Web Working Group provided her initial guidance. A fellow member of that group, Steve Baskauf (now Librarian for Data Curation and Data Science at the Vanderbilt University Libraries), developed a prototype application with her data using linked data principles. But the current application came together when Miller adopted the Srophe platform being developed by David Michelson, Associate Professor of the History of Christianity in the Divinity School, and colleagues.

In "Using XQuery and XSLT to Build an Aggregation of Metadata Records for Religious Texts and Non-Print Items," Christian Schwartz, Systems and Electronic Resources Librarian at Princeton Theological Seminary, describes the process of building the Theological Commons. The Theological Commons now numbers among the largest open access databases of religious and theological texts. Like any new venture, the Theological Commons emerged from the alchemy of risk and faith. The small team of librarians that collaborated on the project was not trained professional programmers. As Schwartz notes, she transitioned from her role as Head Cataloger, a responsible managerial role in the library, to take on the maverick new position of Metadata Librarian.

The XQuery programming language is a common thread of these two applications. While the database differs–Srophe uses eXistDB, an open-source XML database and the Theological Commons is built on MarkLogic, a commercial application–both use XQuery as an application language. As part of her shift to metadata work, Schwartz learned to program in XQuery and, later, XSLT. For the majority of software engineers, these are abstruse technologies best avoided in favor of mainstream languages like C#, JavaScript, and Python. But, as she documents, XQuery and XSLT excel in the transformation of XML metadata, which remain the *lingua franca* of library metadata. Schwartz's essay demonstrates how the core competencies of librarianship persist in the digital humanities while finding new expression. What differs is the need to identify or invent new data models, to transfer data between formats, and to link data together in novel ways. Librarianship shone in developing shared models of cataloging and metadata description in order to facilitate standards for description and access. XML, XSLT, and XQuery provide a welcome complement to AACR2, RDA, BIBFRAME, and the like as technologies based on standards (primarily, at the W3C). Implicitly, Schwartz makes a strong case for this XML-based stack as an alternative platform for describing, manipulating, and querying metadata.

Digital Humanities Pedagogy

Reading the contributions to this volume invariably raises feelings of inadequacy and imposter syndrome. Library science and doctoral programs in the humanities did not train students in the digital humanities until recently. For the most part, digital humanists trained themselves in the metadata standards, programming languages, databases, and application frameworks that undergird their projects. They also learned enough about project management and software engineering to develop and sustain teams when necessary. As their ambitions became more sophisticated, digital humanists also bridged the "two cultures," joining their expertise in their fields of humanistic inquiry with subjects like linear algebra, statistics, and discrete mathematics. In the early days of the digital humanities, advisors and chairs not uncommonly regarded these activities as distractions from research their graduate students and assistant professors should be pursuing.

For librarians, the transition to digital humanities came more easily in certain respects. Natural connections exist between librarianship and information science, on the one hand, and computer science and software engineering, on the other. For library professionals like Schwartz, identifying those analogies paved the way for moving from managing a cataloging workflow to collaborating on a software platform as a member of a digital scholarship team. But there was also much that was new. If my experience running digital scholarship events at Vanderbilt University is representative, digital scholarship librarians learned by proposing workshops on topics of campus interest–data visualization, geospatial information systems, podcasting, network analysis, source control, etc.–and then worked overtime reading, watching YouTube videos, and trying (and failing) to set up demonstration applications in the weeks before their presentations. As librarians strive to cover the gaps in their own training and experience, they also help to fill curricular gaps in college, university, and seminary programs.

The go-go days of digital humanities training are coming to a close as the field matures, professionalizes, and develops more formal programs of instruction. In some seminaries and divinity schools, librarians continue to supplement the formal course of instruction with both credit-bearing and noncredit classes in digital humanities. In other contexts, librarians collaborate with faculty in the teaching of digital humanities coursework. Whatever the modality, librarians are becoming more sophisticated in their understanding of digital humanities pedagogy.

Richard Manly Adams, Jr., exemplifies this emerging sophistication in "Defining Digital Pedagogy in Theological Libraries." Adams, who is Director of Pitts Theology Library and Assistant Professor in the Practice of Theological Bibliography at the Chandler School, calls for instruction that flows from a full-orbed vision of critical digital pedagogy, embracing both new methods and new tools, but eschewing novelty as an end-in-itself. Borrowing a term from John Russell and Merinda Kaye Hensley, Adams contends that mere "buttonology" shortchanges students by showcasing new technologies out of scholarly context and suggesting, by extension, that they can formulate and solve questions in the digital humanities purely instrumentally. This kind of instrumentalist pedagogy mirrors the so-called "technological solutionism" that Evgeny Morozov lampoons in *To Save Everything, Click Here*.[4]

As an alternative to walking students through "point and click" examples, Adams provides a series of rubrics for critical digital literacy instruction. He counsels connecting digital scholarship instruction with activities in the classroom as well as in the library. By way of their position as scholar-practitioners of digital scholarship in the academy, librarians have the opportunity to transfer what they learn from their practical activities in building digital archives and libraries to the academic curricula, crafting practical exercises that connect with students' learning goals. But, most importantly, Adams contends that librarians have "a moral obligation" to teach students to think critically about digital tools and methods. By inviting them to reflect critically on the potential impact, both positive and negative, that adoption of technologies may have on the people to whom they minister, he helps them to anticipate what otherwise might retrospectively have been dismissed as unforeseen consequences.

---

4 Evgeny Morozov, *To Save Everything, Click Here: The Folly of Technological Solutionism* (New York: PublicAffairs, 2014).

In the next chapter, Gayathri Narasimham and I also seek to improve the teaching of the digital humanities, drawing on the experience of computer science educators and connecting their hard-won pedagogical expertise to the contextualization of the teaching of computation in the humanities. We describe how our experience teaching The Beauty and Joy of Computing, a curriculum for introductory computer science, combined with the use of NetsBlox, a blocks-based programming environment, inspired us to think differently about digital humanities pedagogy. While students in religious studies and theology come from a variety of backgrounds, they tend to have majored in the humanities as undergraduates and typically approach the digital humanities without much background in computer science. How can we foster a contextual approach that sustains the interest of students by helping them to achieve practical digital goals while also providing them with a strong foundation in computing that they can transfer to other problems and domains? We describe our ongoing efforts to borrow principles from The Beauty and Joy of Computing while adapting NetsBlox into an educational computing platform for the digital humanities.

Collaboration and Beyond

The final chapter in this volume exemplifies the possibility and potential of non-hierarchical collaboration among practitioners of the digital humanities. The Experimental Humanities Lab at Iliff School of Theology is the author of the chapter; the individual contributors cede their contributions to the collective. The practice of collective authorship has a long history, of course. Wikipedia relies on the work of countless volunteers globally who have fused their knowledge and creativity, collaborating, oftentimes quarrelling, always revising, to produce the world's greatest encyclopedia.[5] Still, this level of authorial effacement remains unusual in the digital humanities, serving as a protest against and correction of the kind of self-promotion that mars teamwork in the academy. This renunciation of authorial right allows them to sidestep Turing's question, "Can machines think?" and to invite the machine as a partner in their explorations, expanding their perspective beyond the human to include the alien "mind" of the algorithm.

The members of the Experimental Humanities Lab reinforce the major themes of this volume–interdisciplinarity and partnership–and add another:

---

5 Andrew Lih, *The Wikipedia Revolution: How a Bunch of Nobodies Created the World's Greatest Encyclopedia* (New York: Hyperion, 2009).

the concept of library as interface. By this, they intend that libraries themselves serve as platforms for "probabilistic production," that is, a kind of serendipitous digital discovery that emerges from interdisciplinary and cross-functional encounter. The study of theology and religion flourishes, as it always has, within this shifting dialogue with adjacent and distant disciplines. As they became accustomed to sharing ideas in this unstable dialogic, they also gained facility in translation, inviting new members into their fold, teaching them the rudiments of Python, explaining their interim findings to administrators and funding agencies, and sharing their ideas in drafts of the then-emerging guidelines of the American Academy of Religion for evaluating digital humanities scholarship. This generosity and open-endedness serve as their signature and, they hope, as a hallmark of the ethical practice of digital humanities in the academy.

Digital humanities bear the potential to transform not just research, but the practice of the humanities academy. To a degree, librarians, faculty, and other information professionals have grown accustomed to operating in silos, speaking different disciplinary parlances and aligning their practices with different norms. If nothing else, the chapters in these volumes illustrate that scaling the digital humanities requires all sides to collaborate more closely, less hierarchically, and more generously. As theological libraries retrench and religious studies departments face cuts in the view of tightening socioeconomic circumstances, the digital humanities will not save the theological academy in its present form. But perhaps the practices of digital humanities may foster the emergence of a more interdisciplinary, less hierarchical, more exploratory theological academy in its place.

I Methodological Approaches

Michał Choiński and Jan Rybicki
Puritan Preachers in the Hands of Statisticians: The Stylometric Study of Colonial Religious Writings

1 Introduction

This article presents the overview of an OPUS research project "The Language of Eighteenth-Century American Colonial Sermons. A Rhetorical and Stylometric Analysis" (2014/13/B/HS2/00905), carried out in the Institute of English Studies at the Jagiellonian University. Upon putting together their proposal, the two authors of the project were quite aware, from the very start, that their proposal may raise some eyebrows on both sides of the Atlantic–why should the (predominantly Catholic) Polish taxpayer be asked to fund a venture that would look into the work of the 18th century Puritan preachers from Colonial America? And yet, the Board of Poland's National Science Centre consented to the proposal and agreed to finance the project, which lasted altogether three years (2015–2018), and in which for the first time, in Poland, a quantitative approach to textual material from American early modern letters was applied. This interdisciplinary alliance of two methodologies: the stylometric study of the authorship signal that is part of the much more general field of digital humanities on the one hand, and historical-rhetorical approach to text on the other, demonstrates how the qualitative and quantitative may be reconciled, and how the synthesis of the divine and the digital may contribute to the existing scholarship on colonial religious history.

The purpose of this essay is to present the research approach used in that OPUS project, as well as the overall results of the application of quantitative methods to the corpus of colonial revival sermons, paying particular attention to the oeuvre of Jonathan Edwards, one of the central figures of the first Great Awakening. Three stylometric experiments are described below. In the first one, various texts of a group of colonial preachers are compared and contrasted with the help of stylometric tools to show possible intertextual affinities between particular authors. In the second experiment, the writings of Jonathan Edwards are classified into groups, in connection with how his stylometric signal changed over his life. Finally, applying a similar approach to individual works, the authors of the article study the extent to which Edwards's writings were informed by the style of his editor, Thomas Foxcroft–also, seeking to pinpoint the sections

∂ OpenAccess. © 2021 Michał Choiński and Jan Rybicki, published by De Gruyter. [CC BY-NC-ND] This work is licensed under the Creative Commons Attribution-NonCommercial-NoDerivatives 4.0 International License.
https://doi.org/10.1515/9783110536539-003

of his treatises that were most heavily augmented by Foxcroft (if not written entirely by him).

2 The Stylometric Approach

Stylometry has been used in textual studies even before the advent of computers, mainly in authorship attribution and plagiarism detection[1] but also in Platonic chronology.[2] Stylometric research projects became even easier to conduct with computers;[3] the growing availability of electronic texts triggered a veritable explosion of the field into quantitative literary studies that go beyond authorship[4] and into Distant Reading.[5] In general, stylometry calculates the features of texts —often very simple features, such as word- or character- or part-of-speech-frequencies—and shows the linguistic or indeed stylistic differences between texts, authors, or groups of authors.

The above-cited seminal work by Mosteller and Wallace used function word counts to give a convincing answer to the question of the authorship of pamphlets urging citizens of New York to ratify the Constitution of the United States.[6] Burrows applied an analogous method to show the similarity of frequent-word usage in the idiolects of similar characters in Jane Austen.[7] Hoover demonstrates

---

[1] E.g., Thomas C. Mendenhall, "A Mechanical Solution of a Literary Problem," *The Popular Science Monthly*, 1903.

[2] Wincenty Lutosławski, *The Origin and Growth of Plato's Logic: With an Account of Plato's Style and of the Chronology of His Writings* (London: Longmans, Green, and Co., 1897).

[3] E.g., Frederick Mosteller and David L. Wallace, *Inference and Disputed Authorship* (Reading, MA: Addison-Wesley, 1964).

[4] E.g., John Frederick Burrows, *Computation Into Criticism: A Study of Jane Austen's Novels and an Experiment in Method* (Oxford: Clarendon Press, 1987); David L. Hoover, "A Conversation Among Himselves: Change and the Styles of Henry James," in *Digital Literary Studies: Corpus Approaches to Poetry, Prose, and Drama*, ed. David L. Hoover, Jonathan Culpeper, and Kieran O'Halloran (New York and London: Routledge, 2014), 90–119; Jan Rybicki, "The Great Mystery of the (Almost) Invisible Translator: Stylometry in Translation," in *Quantitative Methods in Corpus-Based Translation Studies: A Practical Guide to Descriptive Translation Research*, ed. Michael P. Oakes and Ji Meng (Amsterdam: John Benjamins Publishing Company, 2012), 231–48; and Jan Rybicki, "Vive La Différence: Tracing the (Authorial) Gender Signal by Multivariate Analysis of Word Frequencies," *Digital Scholarship in the Humanities* 31, no. 4 (2015): 746–61, https://doi.org/10.1093/llc/fqv023.

[5] Matthew L. Jockers, *Macroanalysis: Digital Methods and Literary History* (Urbana: University of Illinois Press, 2013).

[6] Mosteller and Wallace, *Inference and Disputed Authorship*.

[7] Burrows, *Computation Into Criticism*.

a very clear evolution of frequent-word frequencies throughout the *oeuvre* of Henry James.[8] The same frequencies seem to preserve the signal of the original author rather than the translator in literary translations;[9] medium frequency words, on the other hand, are good indicators of authorial gender.[10] Jockers' work explores the various stylometric signals in large textual corpora, seeking to investigate entire literary traditions, and thus asking questions that cannot be readily answered by traditional close reading.[11] The authors of this article themselves have applied the stylometric method for the study of American literature–among others, to discuss the authorship of Harper Lee's second novel, *Go Set a Watchman*, when its much-awaited release was surrounded by controversy.[12] Many more examples could be mentioned here; indeed, the field has produced a good volume of compelling empirical data–and relatively little by way of theoretical basis for the results. The one consensus is that "the possibility of using frequency patterns of very common words (may) rest upon the fact that words do not function as discrete entities. Since they gain their full meaning through the different sorts of relationship they form with each other, they can be seen as markers of those relationships and, accordingly, of everything that those relationships entail."[13]

One of the standard procedures in stylometry by most frequent words serves as the basis for a software package, "stylo,"[14] written for R, the open-source statistical programming environment.[15] For the research procedure to be carried out, the first thing needed, of course, is a collection of texts. In the case of this study, the writings by Jonathan Edwards constituted the core of the studied material. For the purpose of this OPUS project, access to the complete collection of works authored by the Northampton minister was offered by the Jonathan Ed-

---

[8] Hoover, "A Conversation Among Himselves: Change and the Styles of Henry James."
[9] Rybicki, "The Great Mystery of the (Almost) Invisible Translator: Stylometry in Translation."
[10] Rybicki, "Vive La Différence."
[11] Jockers, *Macroanalysis*.
[12] Jan Rybicki, Maciej Eder, and Michał Choiński, "Harper Lee and Other People: A Stylometric Diagnosis," *The Mississippi Quarterly* 70–71, no. 3 (June 22, 2017): 355–75.
[13] Wayne Mckenna, John Burrows, and Alexis Antonia, "Beckett's Trilogy: Computational Stylistics and the Nature of Translation," *Revue Informatique et Statistique Dans Les Sciences Humaines* 35, no. 1–4 (1999): 152.
[14] Maciej Eder, Jan Rybicki, and Mike Kestemont, "Stylometry with R: A Package for Computational Text Analysis," *The R Journal* 8, no. 1 (2016).
[15] R Core Team, *R: A Language and Environment for Statistical Computing*, 2014, http://www.R-project.org/.

wards Center at Yale University;[16] the writings of other early modern authors were also used for comparison; these were extracted from Early American Imprints. Once such a corpus of texts was produced in electronic form, the frequencies of all the words were counted, first in the corpus, then in all individual texts. In this way, the selection of the words used in the experiment (usually, the first 100, the first 200, the first 300, etc.) is not performed by the researcher; instead, it is established by the corpus itself. In most English texts, the first five of these MFWs will invariably include *the*, *to*, and *and* and only very small differences in frequency rank will be observed between their usage in individual texts; but it is through those small differences that a surprising amount of comparative information is often revealed.

Of course, these numbers are not yet useful for any comparison, since they constitute raw rather than relative values. They must now be made relative to the size of each text. The easiest way to do so would be to divide each word-type frequency count by the size, in word tokens, of each text, and this was the approach applied by Burrows in his above-cited Jane Austen study; later on, however, he produced a more sophisticated formula that converted such raw word frequencies into a measure of distance (or dissimilarity) between texts. Indeed, Burrows's Delta distance became a standard in stylometry.[17] Thus, for two texts, T and T1, and for a set of n words, the distance (the degree of similarity/difference) between them is calculated as

$$\Delta(T, T_1) = \frac{1}{n}\sum_{x=1}^{n} |z(f_i(T)) - z(f_i(T_1))|$$

where

$$z(f_x(T)) = \frac{f_x(T) - \mu_x}{\sigma_x}$$

where, in turn,
$f_x(T)$ = raw frequency of word x in text T;
μ_x = mean frequency of word x in a collection of texts;
σ_x = standard deviation of frequency of word x.

---

16 The authors of the article would like to use this opportunity to express their gratitude to Prof. Kenneth Minkema, the director of the Jonathan Edwards Center at Yale University for his willingness to share the edited corpus of Jonathan Edwards's writings.
17 John Burrows, "'Delta': A Measure of Stylistic Difference and a Guide to Likely Authorship," *Literary and Linguistic Computing* 17, no. 3 (September 1, 2002): 267–87, https://doi.org/10.1093/llc/17.3.267.

To express this in words rather than in algebra, Delta is the mean of the absolute differences between the z-scores for a set of word-variables in a given text-group and the z-scores for the same set of word-variables in a target text. This is obviously a much better distance measure since, by inserting mean frequencies and standard deviations, one can arrive at a much better account of the frequency distributions in the texts studied than mere relative frequencies. When strings of frequencies are compared between all the texts in a set, this produces another table, which contains the Delta distances between each pair of texts, not unlike a table of distances between cities at the back of a country's road atlas. Just as such a table would provide the distance between, say, New York and Washington, D.C., the table now shows, in a numerical fashion, the distance (or the degree of dissimilarity), between each pair of texts in the corpus. Indeed, just as these distances between American cities could be used by statistical methods to reproduce the general shape of the U.S., sets of distances between texts help classify and organize individual texts in relation to each other on graphs.

At this point, various statistic methods can help to visualize such a system of distances. One of these is Cluster Analysis. It compares strings of numbers denoting the distances between the individual texts that cluster around the nearest neighbours (texts) on branches of a tree diagram. The existing literature shows that this works for most (literary) texts in most languages[18]–at least where the strongest signal, that of authorship attribution, is concerned.

Sometimes, however, minor differences may appear between results obtained for different sizes of the most-frequent-word list; for instance, results for the first 100 words can be identical with those for the first 200 words; but then slight changes may start appearing with increasing wordlist length. There is a way around this dilemma–Cluster Analysis is performed for various wordlist sizes and the results are pooled in what is a called a Bootstrap Consensus. This method only shows the strongest connections between the texts in the corpus. Still, both Cluster Analysis and its Bootstrap Consensus share a common drawback. Namely, they only provide binary answers, like text A is closest to text B; text C is closest to text D, etc. Such an outcome does not say much about the degree of similarity or difference between A and C, and B and D. And, obviously, such an outcome is not satisfactory in literary or historical studies. For instance, one author can be similar almost equally to two different authors, and this might not show up in the diagram produced. Luckily, network analysis, using software

---

18 For a comparative study of this phenomenon, see Maciej Eder and Jan Rybicki, "Do Birds of a Feather Really Flock Together, or How to Choose Training Samples for Authorship Attribution," *Literary and Linguistic Computing* 28, no. 2 (June 1, 2013): 229–36, https://doi.org/10.1093/llc/fqs036.

such as Gephi[19] can produce diagrams that preserve all signals—not just the strongest one. And this is exactly how the research conducted under the auspices of the OPUS grant was carried out. This procedure, from electronic text input to obtaining network analysis graphs, is most comprehensively described and discussed by Eder.[20]

3 The Historical Context

A larger part of the corpus of texts studied in the OPUS project is connected with the Great Awakening (1739–1745), the first mass-scale Puritan revival of America. During that time, building upon a series of revivals from the mid-1730s, a group of itinerant preachers was able to impact crowds of thousands of people, instigating emotional reactions which often bordered on mass hysteria. This propelled the development of new forms of preaching, which manifested the power of the spoken word to colonists and fuelled the public debate.[21] This context accounts for why the project's corpus consisted predominantly of sermons.

In colonial communities, sermons played a significant role, both social and religious. As observed by Harry Stout,[22] they were the mass media of the period and functioned as the only regular medium of social debate. It is calculated that during the entire colonial period, when the population of colonies never reached beyond 1.5 million and in the largest city, Boston, lived 17,000 inhabitants, almost 5 million sermons were delivered. Preaching permeated the culture of the time and reflected the current social, intellectual, religious, and political debates.

Also, the Great Awakening impacted the colonial print culture. With the ongoing discussion about the status and the ramifications of the Great Awakening for the spiritual and public functioning of the colonies, a plethora of publications appeared. The most vitriolic debate erupted between the Old Lights (the critics of the revival) and the New Lights (its proponents). Little wonder that

---

19 Mathieu Bastian, Sebastien Heymann, and Mathieu Jacomy, "Gephi: An Open Source Software for Exploring and Manipulating Networks," in *Proceedings of the International AAAI Conference on Web and Social Media*, vol. 3:1, 2009.
20 Maciej Eder, "Does Size Matter? Authorship Attribution, Small Samples, Big Problem," *Digital Scholarship in the Humanities* 30, no. 2 (2015): 167–82.
21 Cf. Michał Choiński, *The Rhetoric of the Revival: The Language of the Great Awakening Preachers* (Göttingen: Vandenhoeck & Ruprecht, 2016).
22 Harry S. Stout, *The New England Soul: Preaching and Religious Culture in Colonial New England* (New York: Oxford University Press, 1986), 3.

in the second half of the twentieth century, a number of commentators began approaching the revival also as a critical historical event that informed the American Revolution,[23] shaped colonial culture and aesthetics[24] as well as the significance of religion in the society.[25] Also, literature on the silhouettes of the key proponents of the Great Awakening has grown opulent in the last four decades and the life and output of such preachers as Jonathan Edwards,[26] George Whitefield[27] or Gilbert Tennent[28] were discussed.

Surprisingly, until recently, only a few of these studies investigated the language-related aspects of colonial revivalism. In his article surveying different publications on the Great Awakening, Guelzo observed that "the rhetorical meanings of the Awakening are far from well understood."[29] The idea to analyse the texts of sermons stylometrically was a chance for a better understanding of linguistic aspects of the revival and the communicative mechanisms employed by the preachers to propagate the idea of the "New Birth." Most importantly, such an approach can empirically determine the connections between the styles of particular preachers and yield results that could not be obtained by manual analysis, driven only by the naked human eye.

The OPUS research grant reported on in this essay is not the only DH project dedicated to the study of the colonial religious discourse. For instance, in his research on Edwards, Rob Boss uses exegetic visualizations to study the interrelations between various theological concepts in the preacher's "Miscellanies." Boss's "Miscellanies Project" (2018), carried out with JESociety, aims to create a library of visualizations which comprehensively map theological topics found in Edwards's notebooks and the rest of the Yale letterpress edition of *The Works of Jonathan Edwards*. These network maps can be dynamically ex-

---

[23] Alan Heimert, *Religion and the American Mind: From the Great Awakening to the Revolution* (Cambridge: Harvard University Press, 1966).
[24] Edwin S. Gaustad, *The Great Awakening in New England* (New York: Harper, 1957); Cedric B. Cowing, *The Great Awakening and the American Revolution: Colonial Thought in the 18th Century* (New York: Rand McNally, 1971).
[25] Mark A. Noll, *The Rise of Evangelicalism: The Age of Edwards, Whitefield and the Wesleys* (Downers Grove: InterVarsity Press, 2003).
[26] E. g., George M. Marsden, *Jonathan Edwards: A Life* (New Haven: Yale University Press, 2003).
[27] Harry S. Stout, *The Divine Dramatist: George Whitefield and the Rise of Modern Evangelicalism* (Grand Rapids: Wm. B. Eerdmans Publishing Co., 1991).
[28] Milton J. Coalter, *Gilbert Tennent, Son of Thunder: A Case Study of Continental Pietism's Impact on the First Great Awakening in the Middle Colonies* (New York: Greenwood Press, 1986).
[29] Allen Guelzo, "God's Designs: The Literature of the Colonial Revival of Religion, 1735–1760," in *New Directions in American Religious History*, ed. Harry S. Stout and D.G. Hart (New York: Oxford University Press, 1997), 162.

plored, annotated, and animated with the accompanying JEViewer software and its Zoom interface. JEViewer also enables easy data exchange between users so that they can share annotations and graphical views. Such digital exegesis is but one of numerous examples of how DH methodologies can contribute to the existing scholarship on early modern religious discourse.

4 Stylometric Network of Colonial Preachers

The first experiment conducted as part of the OPUS research grant consisted in the comparative study of a group of preachers: Solomon Stoddard (1643–1729), Samuel Sewall (1652–1730), Benjamin Colman (1673–1747), Thomas Prince (1687–1758), Jonathan Dickinson (1688–1747), Nathaniel Appleton (1693–1784), Jonathan Edwards (1703–1758), Gilbert Tennent (1703–1764), Jonathan Parsons (1705–1776), Eleazar Wheelock (1711–1779), George Whitefield (1717–1770), Joseph Bellamy (1719–1790) and Ezra Stiles (1727–1797). All the preachers selected for this preliminary study were connected with the Great Awakening–either by being its active participants and later defendants, or by instigating the pre-revival "harvests" of conversions in the Connecticut River Valley in the 1730s. For the purpose of this initial experiment, plain text files with collections of their sermons were prepared–in the cases of preachers, whose writings were particularly extensive (in Figure 1, this concerns Whitefield and Edwards), these were divided into smaller collections, respective of the decades when the given sets of sermons were delivered.

Figure 1 demonstrates, among other things, the extent to which the sermons of Edwards and Stoddard, Edwards's grandfather, show stylometric resemblance. Such a statistically-derived result is hardly surprising from the perspective of qualitative analysis. Sweeney points out that Stoddard "cast[s] a mighty long shadow over Edwards' ministry"[30] and his impact on the young Jonathan's "ministry of words" was formative. Stoddard, dubbed the "Pope" of the Connecticut River Valley, gained repute as an uncompromising revivalist who preached hellfire, and who, at the same time, demonstrated a liberal approach in the controversy over the Half-Way Covenant. In 1725, Jonathan Edwards received a proposal to become an assistant to Stoddard, and, upon the latter's death in 1729, took over the Northampton congregation. Edwards did not approve of Stoddard's leniency over the admission to church membership and the sacrament of the

---

[30] Douglas A. Sweeney, *Jonathan Edwards and the Ministry of the Word: A Model of Faith and Thought* (Downers Grove: InterVarsity Press, 2009), 34.

Lord's Supper, and swiftly implemented much stricter rules in this respect; in terms of preaching, however, he looked up to the authority and rhetorical prowess commanded by his grandfather with great reverence.

Curiously, the software placed Appleton's late sermons and Dickinson's early sermons not far away from the Edwards-Stoddard cluster. And, the late discourses of Parsons, Wheelock, and Stiles were put relatively close to one another. Such empirical results encourage a direct comparative reading of sermons by these authors, seeking to explain the affinity of stylometric signals by the investigation of the rhetorical mechanisms they employ. Likewise, the significant resemblance between the stylometric signals of Parsons, Prince, Stiles, and Wheelock detected by the software encourages a closer comparative study of the sermons by these preachers.

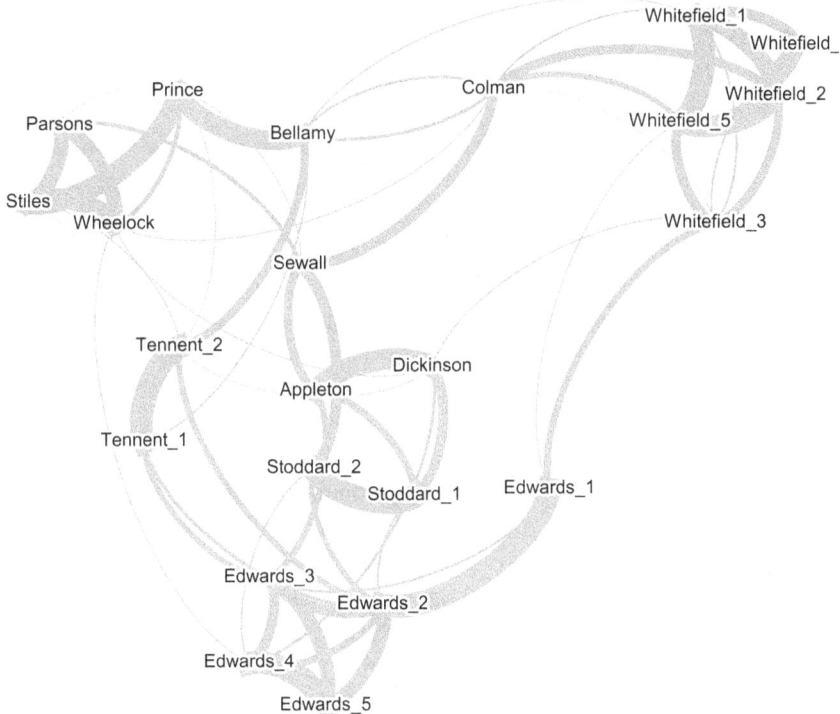

Figure 1: Network analysis showing stylometric differences between a group of American colonial preachers regarding the most-frequent-word usage.

Not all results presented in *Figure 1* are equally unexpected. For instance, Whitefield's numerous sermons constitute a network cluster far removed from that of

Edwards and Stoddard. The readers acquainted with the Great Awakening sermons should not be surprised by such an outcome. Although Edwards and Whitefield are, arguably, the most recognizable figures of the Great Awakening and remain most directly associated with the revival enthusiasm of the 1740s in the Colonies, their sermons are completely dissimilar. Whitefield, as a "divine dramatist,"[31] was famous for his pulpit performance, and relied predominantly on preaching theatrics for his communicative success. His sermons abound in dialogues, evocative rhetorical figures, and organizational structures that remind one of theatre. Edwards, on the other hand, is a painter of words—for whom the theological message framed in elaborate tropological structures would become the recognized rhetorical trademark–as argued by Turnbull, "by Puritan standards Edwards's sermons are works of art."[32]

5 Stylometric Study of Edwards's Corpus

For the purpose of the second experiment, the complete corpus of Edwards's texts was divided into groups that follow the division of volumes introduced by the Yale editors of the *Complete Works of Jonathan Edwards*. Next, the files were labeled in such a way as to allow for a clear interpretation of the results on the diagram. The key phrases point to titles (e.g., *Affections* stands for the treatise *Religious Affections*), single capitals signal the genre of the texts (T stands for treatises, L for letters and S for sermons), and, finally, dates point to the publication year. The greatest interest of a stylometric study on such a corpus was to see whether most-frequent-word usage might reflect the traditional division, and to check if indeed, as argued by the editors of his texts, "his sermons reflect the stages of his busy life."[33]

In Figure 2, one can clearly see that the stylometric survey of our Edwards corpus revealed five distinct groups of writings. The first cluster (C1) of texts visible in the top left part of the diagram includes Edwards's letters and private writings. Interestingly, here, his *Personal Narrative*, as well as *The Life of David Brainerd* (Edwards's biography of an early 18th century missionary to the Native Americans) turn out to be the most remote from the rest of the corpus. Slightly less distinct, drifting gradually towards other groups, are family letters and cor-

---

31 Cf. Stout, *The Divine Dramatist*.
32 Ralph G. Turnbull, *Jonathan Edwards: The Preacher* (Grand Rapids: Baker Book House, 1958), 44.
33 Wilson H. Kimnach, Kenneth P. Minkema, and Douglas A. Sweeney, eds., *The Sermons of Jonathan Edwards: A Reader* (New Haven: Yale University Press, 1999), 1.

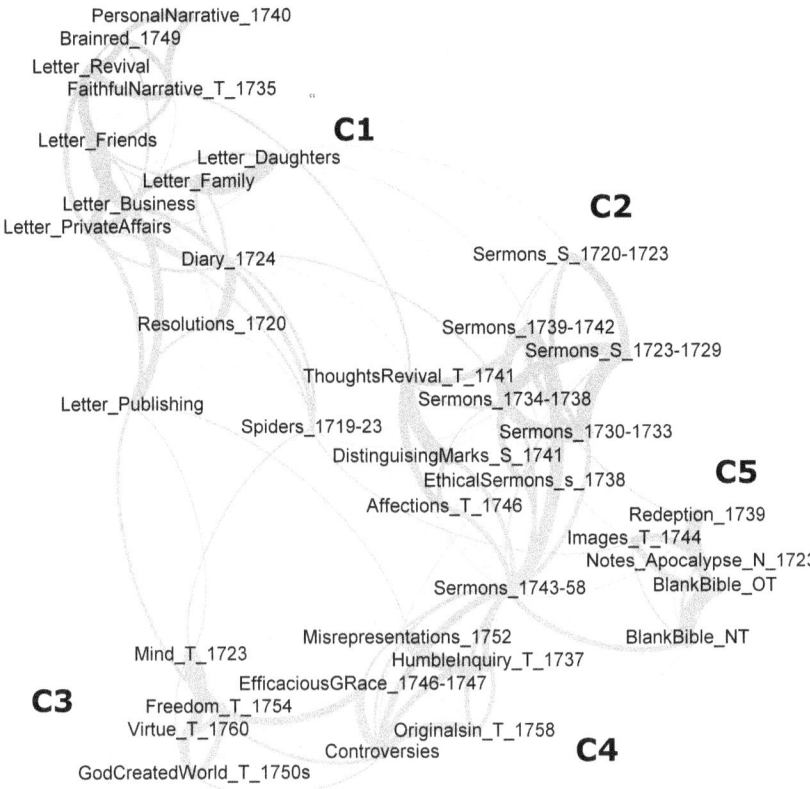

Figure 2: Network analysis of most-frequent-word usage in the works of Jonathan Edwards.

respondence concerning his business and publishing affairs. Also, Edwards's early account of the Northampton revival was incorporated into this cluster. Thus, in terms of the stylometric signal, the "private" Edwards communicating his common problems and concerns, using ordinary, concrete phrases, coalesces with the "pulpit" Edwards, describing religious experiences, and becomes distinctively separate from the "public" Edwards of his other published writings.

The whole C1 cluster also seems to be separate in terms of genre, as most of the elements incorporated into this first group are epistolary texts. One can argue that it is not only that Edwards's language used for writing about his personal affairs is distinct from the language he employed in his pulpit oratory, but also the sheer convention of letter-writing dictated the employment of different sets of vocabulary or syntax and contributed to this group's visibly salient character. The letters most removed from the group are the ones Edwards exchanged in connection with his publishing plans, mainly with Thomas Foxcroft, his editor. Here, the language employed by the preacher, on account of him making references to the texts he was working on in the publication process, understandably drives the epistles towards the said publications. At the same time, Edwards's *Diary*, his writings on spiders, as well as *Resolutions*—all three being some of the earliest texts in the whole corpus—although ranked in this first group, seem to drift to the right of the diagram, in the direction of other clusters, forming a bridge between the "private" Edwards and Edwards's second distinct group of texts (C2).

This second cluster of Edwards's writings also bears distinct genre marking, as it is comprised almost exclusively of his sermons. The pulpit oratory of the Northampton minister constitutes the most prominent element of the corpus, both in terms of the number of publications as well as their significance. At the same time, it is this cluster that allows one to look into the chronological changes in Edwards's writing and to trace the evolution of his written word. Edwards's earliest sermons, written between 1720–1723, are the most remote from the group, as they gravitate towards the top of the diagram, away from all the other texts. This, however, changes when one looks at his later writings. Other sermonic elements of the corpus, written in the successive time periods, gradually drift towards its center, allowing us to see the chronological sequence: sermons dating to 1723–1729 follow the earliest collection of texts, and are set adjacent to those from 1739–1742, the time of the initial stage of the Great Awakening. The sermons of 1730–1733 disrupt the clear chronology (as ideally they should have followed the 1723–1729 group), but at the same time they bear a direct individual connection to the pulpit oratory from before that period. At the same time, the groups of sermons from 1734–1738 and the Great Awakening discourses drift towards the location between the outermost elements of groups, revealing a discernible stylometric resemblance.

There are two texts which disrupt the otherwise homogenously sermonic character of the C2 cluster: *Thoughts Concerning the Revival* and *Religious Affections*. One would expect them to appear in the treatise groups; it turns out that in terms of the stylometric signal, both these texts more closely resemble Edwards's pulpit oratory than the language employed in his treatises. The theme they touch upon may be partially responsible for their location on the stylometric diagram. Since these two publications of Edwards are thematically connected with the Great Awakening, it is hardly surprising that they exhibit such strong connections with other texts on revivalism, such as the awakening sermons. On the other hand, the sheer thematic resemblance cannot sufficiently explain their location on the diagram. It would seem that Edwards indeed had a unique manner of writing about the religious awakening, and the "rhetoric of the revival"[34] he employed to discuss the mass conversions through the "New Birth," as well as religion directed by affections, leaves a traceable stylometric fingerprint. Edwards's *Ethical Sermons* was also ranked into this group, relatively close to his treatise on religious affections, as well as *Distinguishing Marks*, a treatise-like sermon that constitutes perhaps the most powerful endorsement of colonial revivalism.

There is one small group of sermons that drifts away from the center of the preaching cluster, namely Edwards's pulpit discourses published between 1743–1758. These late sermons visibly diverge towards the stylometric signal of philosophical and theological writings, nonetheless retaining a strong, individual link with the collection of sermons of the Great Awakening, published between 1739–1742 (thus reflecting their chronological affinity). This can be read as a signal that just as the earlier revival sermons exhibited links to Great Awakening writings, so the mature sermons bear a stylistic affinity to the philosophical texts written by Edwards in the same period of time. The stylometric results might then suggest that the extensive work on the publications Edwards was preparing for printing visibly impacted his sermon-writing and would thus explain the evolution of his preaching style.

In spite of the fact that both the clusters of letters (C1) and sermons (C2) include elements that are not representative of the genre (e.g., *Faithful Narrative* for letters and personal writings, and *Thoughts Concerning the Revival* for sermons), there is a distinct stylometric signal of the "pulpit" Edwards and the "private" Edwards. The former, however, seems more distinct, as most elements within this cluster are placed relatively close on the stylometric diagram, and there are strong individual connections between the constituent elements of the group (e.g., between sermons dating to 1730–1733 and 1739–1743 or 1734–1738 and 1723–1729). Also, the stylometry of the preaching texts clearly exhibits a chronological progression in the evolution of Edwards's sermon-writing, as over the years they seem to become gradually more and more treatise-like.

Other writings by Edwards do not exhibit such uniformity or chronological arrangement; in terms of the stylometric signal, Edwards's treatises can be divided into two small sub-clusters. One of them (C3) incorporates his early *The Mind* and some monumental works he wrote during his mission in Stockbridge: *Freedom of the Will*, *The Nature of True Virtue*, and *The Reason Why God Created the World*. The other one (C4) includes *Original Sin* (also completed at Stockbridge), *Efficacious Grace*, *Controversies*, and *An Humble Inquiry*.

---

34 Cf. Choiński, *The Rhetoric of the Revival*, 216.

The last cluster of Edwards's texts (C5) that have their own distinct stylometric signal include such writings as *Notes on Redemption*, *Images of Divine Things* or *The Blank Bible*. These texts seem to distance themselves from his other philosophical and theological writings, and gravitate towards Edwards's sermons on the one hand, and, on the other, towards his biblical commentaries. At the same time, they retain a salient stylometric signal, proving there is a stylistic affinity between them, perhaps conditioned by their intertextual connections with Scripture.

6 Thomas Foxcroft and Jonathan Edwards

The third experiment conducted as part of the OPUS research grant consists in the study of the extent to which Jonathan Edwards's writings were informed by his literary agent and editor, Thomas Foxcroft.[35] Such a discussion aligns well with the renewed interest in Edwards not only as a theologian, but also as an American author functioning within colonial print culture. Some recent studies—Peter J. Thuesen's examination of Edwards's book collection[36] (2008), Wilson Kimnach and Kenneth Minkema's comprehensive study[37] of Edwards's writing process, and Jonathan M. Yeager's investigation[38] of Edwards in the context of the contemporary book market—prove that there is yet a lot to be told about the quotidian functioning of religious writings for American colonies.

This time, the measurement of the respective strength of the stylometric signals of Edwards and Foxcroft focused on individual works to find out which portions retain the stylometric thumbprint of the former, and which exhibit patterns of most-frequent-word usage more characteristic of his editor. This procedure, first described by Eder,[39] relies on samples from the two authors' individual

---

35 An extended version of our research has been published with a special issue of *Amerikastudien*, dedicated to the application of Digital Humanities to American Studies (Choiński, Rybicki 2018). The overview below demonstrates one element of the full study and concerns only one book by Edwards, *The Humble Enquiry*.
36 Peter J. Thuesen, "Introduction," in *The Works of Jonathan Edwards*, ed. Peter J. Thuesen, vol. 26 (New Haven: Yale University Press, 2008), 1–113.
37 Wilson H. Kimnach and Kenneth P. Minkema, "The Material and Social Practices of Intellectual Work: Jonathan Edwards's Study," *The William and Mary Quarterly* 69, no. 4 (2012): 683–730, https://doi.org/10.5309/willmaryquar.69.4.0683.
38 Jonathan M. Yeager, *Jonathan Edwards and Transatlantic Print Culture* (New York: Oxford University Press, 2016).
39 Maciej Eder, "Rolling Stylometry," *Digital Scholarship in the Humanities* 31, no. 3 (September 1, 2016): 457–69, https://doi.org/10.1093/llc/fqv010.

works and compares these to 5000-word sections[40] of those texts by Edwards which are known to have been edited and/or published by Foxcroft.

Historical evidence strongly encourages such investigation. During his service in Northampton and Stockbridge, Edwards relied on Foxcroft's expertise as an editor and literary agent for many of his canonical works, like *An Humble Inquiry* (1749), *Freedom of the Will* (1754), and *Original Sin* (1758). Edwards placed great trust in Foxcroft's erudition and skill to carry out corrections as he intended them. As Yeager emphasizes, when one considers "Edwards's meticulous nature and high standards, it is remarkable how liberal was the dose of trust and flexibility that he dished out to his friend when it came to overseeing the publication of his manuscripts."[41] Edwards's editor sometimes implemented his corrections verbatim, exactly as indicated by the author; at other times, he paraphrased them while preserving what he believed to be the author's idea. Also, Foxcroft's assistance was not limited to the editing of the manuscript only—Edwards entrusted him also with supervision of the entire publication process.

Thus, given the close and prolonged nature of their cooperation, Foxcroft's impact on Edwards's writings demands a detailed investigation—in which the means offered by DH can be of considerable help. Thus, *An Humble Inquiry*, a text known to be the object of their cooperation, was selected as the object of inquiry for the third experiment. The manuscript of this text was written by Edwards in the spring of 1749. It includes a vigorous defence of Edwards's restrictive church policy, which opposed the idea of open church admission propagated by Solomon Stoddard, as mentioned in the previous sections of this essay. The Northampton minister addresses here the arguments of the lenient church thinkers, protesting against the doctrine of visible sainthood his grandfather was an advocate of.

In *An Humble Inquiry*, there are some fragments that exhibit Foxcroft's distinct authorial signal (these are marked light grey in Figure 3). As we discuss in the full report of our research on Edwards and his editor,[42] the first section of the text that can be attributed stylometrically to Foxcroft appears in Part II, beginning with "'Tis evident, that 'tis not only a visibility of moral sincerity in religion . . ." (196), and continues until the paragraph that opens with "But the New Testament affords no more foundation for supposing two real and prop-

---

[40] The length of 5000 words is generally considered promising in terms of statistical significance (cf. Maciej Eder, "Does Size Matter? Authorship Attribution, Small Samples, Big Problem").
[41] Yeager, *Jonathan Edwards and Transatlantic Print Culture*, 96.
[42] Michał Choiński and Jan Rybicki, "Jonathan Edwards and Thomas Foxcroft: Pursuing Stylometric Traces of the Editor," *Amerikastudien* 63, no. 2 (2018): 153.

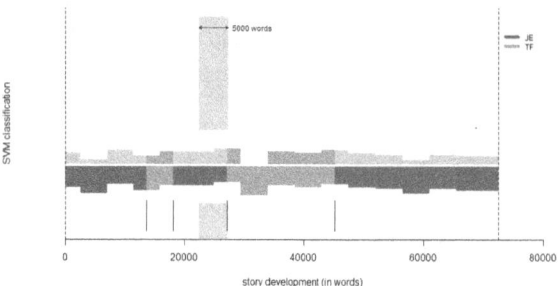

Figure 3: Analysis of "An Humble Inquiry" showing the presence of Foxcroft's stylometric signal in Edwards's text (Edwards: black; Foxcroft: grey). The horizontal line marks the course of the text analysed from the first to the last word. Of the two bands above it, the stronger signal is indicated by the band closer to the axis.

erly distinct covenants of grace, than it does to suppose two sorts of real Christians; the unscripturalness of which latter hypothesis I observed before" (206). The second section potentially 'contaminated' by Foxcroft occurs in the very same part of the treatise, only a few paragraphs later. It begins with the sentence "The same is manifest by the parable of the ten virgins, Matthew 25" (226) and continues to the very beginning of "Part III: Objection Answered." Here, too, stylometric evidence implies that these sections of *An Humble Inquiry* may be attributed to Foxcroft instead of Edwards—or, at least, that the former's editorial changes are so extensive that they heighten his stylistic signal at the expense of the latter's original text. Both above sections support Edwards's agenda, which was also supported by Foxcroft—they are aimed at supporting his claim that only the visible saints should be admitted to the visible church, and that it is the duty of every Christian to seek to maintain the covenant.

In the abundant correspondence between Edwards and his editor, one can find little to explain the latter's presence in the text. In a letter written shortly before *An Humble Inquiry* was to be sent to the printer, Edwards included some last-minute changes to Part III of the manuscript. He also asked Foxcroft to incorporate one fragment into the text, which his editor did, almost verbatim, with minor alterations in punctuation, one minor stylistic alternation of word order, and one change of past tense to present tense: from Stoddard "often taught his people that assurance was attainable" to "often taught his people that assurance is attainable" (*Letters* 287). These alterations could hardly be considered anything more than cosmetic. Thus, the existing correspondence between Edwards and Foxcroft on *An Humble Inquiry* does not account for the strong and consistent presence of the editor's stylometric signal demonstrated in *Figure 3*. The implication is that, perhaps, Foxcroft's alterations were either discussed in correspondence not included in the surviving letters or were unsolicited by the Northampton preacher.

7 Coda

The presentation of the above three experiments is to demonstrate the kind of research that could be conducted with the help of stylometry. In general, the combination of qualitative and quantitative approaches in the OPUS project allowed for a broader outlook on the cultural background of colonial religious discourse—although the results of the research presented above cannot be considered ground-breaking. Still, they were not meant to be. In the case of Jonathan Edwards, the results of this initial stylometric foray make sense when seen in the context of everything that is known, and much indeed is known, of his life and work. Yet there is another end to this stick: since there is so much apparent agreement between the existing biographic/literary/religious/philosophical knowledge on Edwards, the places where stylometry refuses to agree might be worth re-examining by means of traditional scholarship, which might want to explain—to provide but one example—the stylometric migration of some of his sermons towards some of his treatises.

For stylometry must always remember to return to the very texts from which it seems to depart when reaching for mathematical and statistical methods. After all, diagrams of linguistic features alone are irrelevant when dealing with data from the humanities. There is meaning behind the numbers; this meaning must be elicited, and this cannot be done without a marriage of the qualitative with the quantitative. This is why application of statistics to style (or literary history, or genre studies) is best served when the stylometrist collaborates with the literary scholar, the statistician with the historian, in a mood of mutual respect. Thus, apart from the particular collection of texts studied, this project could also constitute an interesting experiment in method. It could help produce the long-awaited connection between traditional literary analysis (such as rhetorical or stylistic) and quantitative tools so far used in linguistics rather than literary studies. In this respect, the project strove to address the problem in a recent paper co-authored by a member of our team, stylometrist Rybicki (but the statement itself came from his co-author, a traditional stylist):

> It seems (that) stylistics should learn how to use the findings of stylometric analysis not only in hope of arriving at some answers but also at new questions; it would help if styl-

ometry could learn to better understand the exact mechanisms that make it so successful a tool of authorial attribution even when the author seems to be concealed by the many possible distortions that translation brings about to word frequencies. And while stylometry and stylistics, despite their similar-sounding names, continue to meet across a deep abyss, this just might be—with a little effort on both sides of the abyss—'the beginning of a beautiful friendship.'[43]

---

[43] Jan Rybicki and Magda Heydel, "The Stylistics and Stylometry of Collaborative Translation: Woolf's Night and Day in Polish," *Literary and Linguistic Computing* 28, no. 4 (December 1, 2013): 708–17, https://doi.org/10.1093/llc/fqt027.

Matthew Handelman
A Messianic Theory of Digital Knowledge: On Positivism and Visualizing Rosenzweig's Archive

> Does not positivism 'reflect' a reality in which man has surrendered to the authority of facts, in which reason, autonomous and critical thinking, is actually subordinate to observation of facts? Does the term 'positive' in positivism not really imply a positive, that is to say, affirmative attitude towards the matters of fact— whatever they might be?
>
> Herbert Marcuse (1941)

Since the 1930s and 1940s, the accusation of positivism has been one of the most severe criticisms in the humanities, as Marcuse's rhetorical questions suggest.[1] For the first generation of critical theorists, the word "positivism" signified the dangerous acceptance and replication of the status quo and, in 1941, the political acquiescence to Nazi totalitarianism as it spread across Europe. In Max Horkheimer and Theodor W. Adorno's *Dialectic of Enlightenment* (1947), the "scientific philosophy" of the logical positivists, a rival school of young philosophers in Vienna, had assumed "the judicial office of enlightened reason" as it returned to the myth and barbarism that was the middle of the past century.[2] Even after the war, positivism remained *persona non grata* in critical theory, as second generation members of the Frankfurt School, such as Jürgen Habermas, adapted and perpetuated the criticisms of the first.[3] With the popularization of big data and

---

[1] Quotation from Marcuse's review of John Dewey's *Theory of Valuation*, which appeared in 1939 in the *International Encyclopedia of Unified Science*, a book series organized by the Vienna Circle; Herbert Marcuse, "Review of John Dewey's Theory of Valuation," *Zeitschrift für Sozialforschung* 9, no. 1 (1941): 145.

[2] Max Horkheimer and Theodor W. Adorno, *Dialectic of Enlightenment*, ed. Gunzelin Schmid Noerr, trans. Edmund Jephcott (Stanford: Stanford University Press, 2002), 19. See also Jürgen Habermas, *Theory of Communicative Action*, trans. Thomas McCarthy, vol. 1 (Boston: Beacon Press, 1984), 22–24.

[3] The dispute between the Frankfurt School and the Vienna Circle before the war set the stage for the so-called "positivism dispute" (*Positivismusstreit*) of the 1960s, between the critical theorists and the critical rationalists, Hans Albert and Karl Popper. For a thorough investigation, see Hans-Joachim Dahms, *Positivismusstreit: Die Auseinandersetzungen der Frankfurter Schule mit*

the digital humanities, positivism has reentered the humanistic milieu as an intellectual slight.[4] And yet critical theory's decades-old antagonism toward scientific rationality (as salient as it may be) has left us with few conceptual tools to approach the digital in the humanities, save to denounce, as Ted Underwood writes, any quantitative, computational, or empirical humanistic work as "positivist."[5] Positivism's return makes one wonder how (or, perhaps, even if) students and scholars, librarians and archivists can employ digital techniques while not only striving for the critical goals, but also practicing the critical methodologies of the humanities.

One answer to this questions lies, as is the contention of this article, in Jewish intellectual life in the German-speaking world during the early twentieth century, which helped give positivism and critical theory the forms in which we recognize them today.[6] The following analysis argues that one of the forerunners of the critical theorists—the German Jewish philosopher, theologian, and translator Franz Rosenzweig—offers inroads for imagining alternative, critical epistemologies in the digital humanities, such as data visualization. Expanding my previous work in visualizing the metadata of Rosenzweig's diasporic archive, I maintain that Rosenzweig's "messianic theory of knowledge" and its idea of "verification" (which I refer to in the German "Bewährung") helps us come to terms with the dual empirical and metaphysical nature of the digital in the humanities.[7] For Rosenzweig, it was the iterative, worldly actions of individuals and groups that, in the course of historical time, "verified" forms of knowledge such

---

dem logischen Positivismus, dem amerikanischen Pragmatismus und dem kritischen Rationalismus (Frankfurt am Main: Suhrkamp Verlag, 1994).

4 See, for instance, Andrew Goldstone, "'Positivist' and Other Terms of Praise," Blog, ARCADE, August 9, 2013, https://arcade.stanford.edu/blogs/positivist-and-other-terms-praise.

5 Underwood tweets: "Dear friends who call all forms of empirical inquiry 'positivism': I have given up trying to nuance your account of history and will instead advance mutual understanding by calling everything you do 'German idealism.'" (@Ted_Underwood), "Dear friends...." Twitter, July 9, 2018, https://twitter.com/ted_underwood/status/1016299439257018369.

6 On the "Jewishness" of the Frankfurt School and the Vienna Circle, see: Jack Jacobs, *The Frankfurt School, Jewish Lives, and Antisemitism* (Cambridge: Cambridge University Press, 2015), chap. 1; Lisa Silverman, *Becoming Austrians: Jews and Culture between the World Wars* (Cambridge: Oxford University Press, 2012), 60–65.

7 This previous work explores the decisions required in extracting and visualizing the metadata contained in the finding aid for Rosenzweig's papers at the University of Kassel. These decisions can be understood as translations and theorized with the help of Rosenzweig's own work on the topic; conversely, the visualizations also reveal larger conversations over Rosenzweig's theory of translation and its relevance for the digital age. Matthew Handelman, "Digital Humanities as Translation: Visualizing Franz Rosenzweig's Archive" 10, no. 1, accessed December 26, 2015, http://transit.berkeley.edu/2015/handelman/.

as religious belief, for which an ultimate, messianic "proof" lay outside of time. My thesis is not that the digital humanities do "Bewährung." Rather, it is that the concept of "Bewährung" mediates between the Absolute and the particular, between the ideal and the real, and, finally, between different modes of knowledge —scientific, philosophical, and religious—in ways that provide an epistemological strategy such that digital humanists might avoid the bland positivism often associated today with the digital.

But what do we mean when we say the word "positivism" and what exactly does it mean to call a digital humanist a "positivist"? Given its modern formulation by Auguste Comte in the nineteenth century, positivism holds that true, "positive" knowledge comes solely from empirical phenomena that are verifiable through sensory experience.[8] The positivist framework continued in the early twentieth century through thinkers like Ernst Mach and the aforementioned Vienna Circle, whose platform of logical positivism held that "there is knowledge only from experience, which rests on what is immediately given" and through the method of "logical analysis."[9] In both positivisms, "positive," verifiable knowledge contrasts what we could call "negative" knowledge in theology and metaphysics, which lacks empirical verification and which the logical positivists rejected as the stuff of "not theory or communication of knowledge [*Wissen*]," but rather "poetry or myth."[10] These positivisms share with debates in the digital humanities a number of laudable scholarly inclinations, such as a dedication to collaborative, cross-disciplinary research.[11] And yet, like the term neoliberalism, positivism has become a catch-all criticism signifying the so-called political "dark side" of digital work, which, according to its critics, eschews critical and historical thought, is subservient to industry, and promotes neoliberalism it-

---

8 On the legacy and reach of Comte and positivism, see Michael Singer, *The Legacy of Positivism* (New York: Palgrave Macmillian, 2005).
9 Anon., "Wissenschaftliche Weltauffassung. Der Wiener Kreis," in Otto Neurath, *Empiricism and Sociology*, ed. Robert S. Cohen and Marie Neurath (Dordrecht: Reidel, 1973), 309. For more on the history and philosophy of logical positivism, see A. J. Ayer, "Editor's Introduction," in *Logical Positivism* (New York: The Free Press, 1966), 3–28; Michael Friedman, *Reconsidering Logical Positivism* (Cambridge: Cambridge University Press, 1999).
10 Anon., "Wissenschaftliche Weltauffassung," 307.
11 The Vienna Circle emphasized the collaborative nature of their work and its interest in the foundations of subjects from arithmetic to the social sciences; Anon., "Wissenschaftliche Weltauffassung," 299 and 310–15. Collaboration and interdisciplinarity have long been central topics in the digital humanities; see, for example, Anne Burdick et al., *Digital_Humanities* (Cambridge: The MIT Press, 2012), 49–51.

self.[12] The universal nature of these criticisms points to a deeper impasse between digital work and critical theories of culture and aesthetics, which, akin to Horkheimer and Adorno, uphold the mismatch of scientific rationality and empirical, data-driven research with the complexity of humanistic inquiry into topics such as art, philosophy, and religious thought.[13] At the risk of reductionism, it is against this ongoing stalemate between the empirical and the metaphysical in the humanities that, so I argue here, Rosenzweig's concept of "Bewährung" stands best poised to intervene.

Reading the visualizations of Rosenzweig's archive through his concept of "Bewährung" responds to ongoing theoretical debates, started by Alan Liu, Johanna Drucker and Lauren Klein, to define critical, humanities-based practices for digital work and to create alternative histories of and epistemologies for data visualization.[14] For instance, Klein's article "The Image of Absence" demonstrates that data visualization holds the potential to render visible "archival silences" and to illuminate these present absences, such as those of James Hem-

---

[12] The "dark side" of the digital humanities refers to a 2013 MLA roundtable, contributions from which appeared in the special issue, "The Shadows of the Digital Humanities," in *differences* (2014) edited by Elizabeth Weed and Ellen Rooney; see also Wendy Hui Kyong Chun et al., "The Dark Side of the Digital Humanities," in *Debates in the Digital Humanities 2016*, ed. Matthew K. Gold and Lauren F. Klein (Minneapolis: University of Minnesota Press, 2016), 493–509. The term "digital positivism" has also become a symbol for the political and social dangers of big data, see Vincent Mosco, *To the Cloud: Big Data in a Turbulent World* (London: Routledge, 2014), chap. 5. The relationship between the digital humanities and neoliberalism has perhaps most forcefully been pointed out by Daniel Allington, Sarah Brouillette, and David Golumbia, "Neoliberal Tools (and Archives): A Political History of Digital Humanities," Los Angeles Review of Books, accessed January 17, 2017, https://lareviewofbooks.org/article/neoliberal-tools-archives-political-history-digital-humanities/.

[13] See, for instance, Tom Eyers, "The Perils of the 'Digital Humanities': New Positivisms and the Fate of Literary Theory," *Postmodern Culture* 23, no. 2 (January 2013), http://www.pomoculture.org/2015/07/08/the-perils-of-the-digital-humanities-new-positivisms-and-the-fate-of-literary-theory/.

[14] Theoretical debates have largely focused on, as Alan Liu put it, the place of cultural criticism in digital work; see "Where Is Cultural Criticism in the Digital Humanities?," in *Debates in the Digital Humanities*, ed. Matthew K. Gold (Minneapolis: University of Minnesota Press, 2012), 490–509. Drucker and Klein's work both propose ways that digital work addresses cultural-critical goals; see, for instance, Johanna Drucker, "Humanities Approaches to Graphical Display," *Digital Humanities Quarterly* 5, no. 1 (2011), http://www.digitalhumanities.org/dhq/vol/5/1/000091/000091.html; Lauren F. Klein, "The Image of Absence: Archival Silence, Data Visualization, and James Hemings," *American Literature* 85, no. 4 (2013): 661–88; Lauren F. Klein, "Feminist Data Visualization; Or, the Shape of History," January 24, 2017, http://lklein.com/conference-papers/feminist-data-visualization-or-the-shape-of-history/.

ings in Thomas Jefferson's papers.¹⁵ Building on such work, I argue that reading images of Rosenzweig's diasporic holdings through the conceptual framework of "Bewährung" draws our attention to the negative underside of each visualization, by reminding us of the not-yet-realized totality hinted at, but not achieved by every "positive" image. True to the prohibition of divine images in Judaism, Rosenzweig's concept of "Bewährung" thus poses a conceptual response to, in the words of the "Manifesto of Modernist Digital Humanities" (2014), the "chauvinist" impulse of positivism, which the logical positivists expressed perhaps best through their claim that "everything is accessible to man" through unified science, which "know[s] *no unsolvable riddle.*"¹⁶ To be sure, Rosenzweig scholars stand to learn a lot in terms of positive knowledge from visualizing archival metadata—from a fuller picture of his intellectual networks to the need to investigate Rosenzweig's underrepresented interlocutors. But these visualizations also teach us that, as critical theory is wrong to dismiss the digital outright, the digital humanities also risk lapsing from criticality to the danger that Marcuse located in positivism the minute they view their method and results as Absolute.

Exploring the uses of library and archival metadata as well as the relevance of the ideas that these data describe, this article argues for the mutual dependence of the empirical-concrete and theoretical-transcendental dimensions of the digital humanities. The following three sections each examine a step in the evolution of the concept of "Bewährung" (representation, temporality, and epistemology) in Rosenzweig's thinking and show how they locate the productive moments of negativity in visualizations of the metadata from Rosenzweig's archival holdings in Germany and the United States.¹⁷ The digital humanities—and, in

---

15 Klein, "The Image of Absence," 665.
16 Alex Christie et al., "Manifesto of Modernist Digital Humanities," hcommons.org, November 14, 2014, http://dx.doi.org/10.17613/M6824T. Anon., "Wissenschaftliche Weltauffassung," 306. Similar utopian and, as criticized by Stanley Fish in *The New York Times*, "messianic" tendencies have characterized debates in and skepticism toward the digital humanities, Stanley Fish, "Mind Your P's and B's: The Digital Humanities and Interpretation," *The New York Times*, January 23, 2012, https://opinionator.blogs.nytimes.com/2012/01/23/mind-your-ps-and-bs-the-digital-humanities-and-interpretation/. For an overview of the link between digital work and utopianism, see Brian Greenspan, "Are Digital Humanists Utopian?," in *Debates in the Digital Humanities 2016*, ed. Matthew K. Gold and Lauren F. Klein (Minneapolis: University of Minnesota Press, 2016), 393–409.
17 The various holdings that make up Rosenzweig's diasporic archive reflect the fate of German Jews fleeing Nazi Germany. The major collections of Rosenzweig's papers and letters are held in the Rosenzweig *Teilnachlass* at the University of Kassel Library, the Papers of Franz Rosenzweig at the Leo Baeck Institute (New York), the Glatzer Collection and Archives at Vanderbilt University, and the Papers of Eugen Rosenstock at Dartmouth University.

particular, library and archival data—have much to offer both Rosenzweig studies and Religious Studies, including broader and more efficient access to the archival record and the computational analysis of texts and metadata. At the same time, ideas usually considered the purview of Religious Studies, such as "Bewährung," will be essential if scholars, librarians, and archivists are to address not only the empirical but also the metaphysical forces at play in the digital humanities.

1 Representation

One could say that the central task of Rosenzweig's thought is to reposition the human as a thinking and existing being at the center of philosophical inquiry. In line with renewed interests in existentialism and esotericism in early-twentieth-century Germany, his magnum opus, *The Star of Redemption* (1921), sought to rescue the individual from obscurity in Hegel's program of Idealism, while maintaining a relationship between human finitude and divine eternity.[18] For Rosenzweig, this relationship is theological, where God, the Absolute, is truth; but, in moves that often seem well ahead of their time, *The Star of Redemption* claims that humans cannot grasp the Absolute as a singular act of thinking and, instead, "have only a share" of the "whole" truth (God) in Christianity and Judaism.[19] As finite beings, we know truth in as much as it can be "be veri-fied, and just in the way in which it is generally denied: namely, by letting the 'whole' truth rest on itself and yet taking the share that we comply with for eternal truth."[20] This passage, to which I will return throughout this section, suggests that the concept of "Bewährung" establishes a link between the transient and the eternal, which is both active and representational to the extent that we

---

[18] Peter Gordon has examined Rosenzweig's relationship to existentialism and other existentialist thinkers, such as Martin Heidegger, in *Rosenzweig and Heidegger: Between Judaism and German Philosophy* (Berkeley: University of California Press, 2003). Benjamin Pollock shows the lasting importance of the Absolute in Rosenzweig's philosophy, Benjamin Pollock, *Franz Rosenzweig and the Systematic Task of Philosophy* (Cambridge: Cambridge University Press, 2009). On the entwinement of aesthetics and mysticism in the early twentieth century, see the canonical work Martina Wagner-Egelhaaf, *Mystik der Moderne: die visionäre Ästhetik der deutschen Literatur im 20. Jahrhundert* (Stuttgart: J.B. Metzler, 1989).
[19] See, for instance, Robert Gibbs, *Correlations in Rosenzweig and Levinas* (Princeton: Princeton University Press, 1992). Franz Rosenzweig, *The Star of Redemption*, trans. Barbara E. Galli (Madison, Wis: University of Wisconsin Press, 2005), 438–39. For the German, see Franz Rosenzweig, *Der Stern der Erlösung*, ed. Reinhold Mayer (Den Haag: Martinus Nijhoff, 1976).
[20] Rosenzweig, *The Star of Redemption*, 416.

"take" a finite portion of the truth in place of an unrealizable whole. There are limitations to Rosenzweig's conceptual language, which regrettably excludes non-Judeo-Christian religions.[21] But the idea of "Bewährung" points to a salient problem recognizable in debates over the digital humanities, namely the ways in which empirical, data-driven research can work in the service of critical goals greater than itself, such as the project of knowledge or ethical action.

But how, exactly, does Rosenzweig envision "Bewährung" working in practice? One clue lies in its etymology. The verb "bewähren" derives from the Old High German "biwāren," which means "to make true, to validate," formed from the adjective "true" ("wahr").[22] "Bewährung" as validation implies making a proposition "true," which can be seen in its usage in criminal justice where to be "auf Bewährung" ("on probation") means to prove through your actions that you are trustworthy; similarly, "Bewährung" was the name the logical positivists gave the process by which theoretical statements are verified by empirical experimentation.[23] In *The Star of Redemption,* the previous passage picks up on these meanings by using the passive without reintroducing an agent in order to emphasize the idea of process. But the text also reimagines "Bewährung" as satisfying two conditions, the first of which requires the here-and-now of my lived experience and worldly action to reflect "the eternal truth" postulated by religious belief. The second condition stipulates that humans recognize that finite beings can never experience "the 'whole' truth" and, hence, not make claims to possess the Absolute in full. For Rosenzweig, this meant that participation in the finite but recurring liturgical cycles upholds the "whole" truth, which gives meaning to my finite existence even as "the 'whole' truth rest[s]" outside of historical experience. The reciprocity of this relationship is what Rosenzweig hints at when he reverses truth as a process of verifying versus denying: rather than the experience of worldly transience precluding the existence of the eternal, human finitude dialectically implies the Absolute. At a historical moment when the Absolute of Hegel's Idealism threatened to erase the individual, "Bewährung" did not reject the Absolute tout court (as would positivism), but rather made the infinite depend on its substantiation in finite experience.

---

21 On this problem, see the contributions to *Rosenzweig Jahrbuch* 2, ed. Martin Brasser.
22 Friedrich Kluge and Elmar Seebold, *Etymologisches Wörterbuch der deutschen Sprache*, 24th ed. (Berlin: De Gruyter, 2002), 118.
23 To avoid the paradoxes associated with common use of the term "true" ("wahr"), Rudolf Carnap proposed the term "verification" as a way of deciding whether to accept or deny the validity of a scientific statement; for Carnap, "verification" occurred by testing statements against empirical observation and comparing them to other known statements. Rudolf Carnap, "Wahrheit und Bewährung," *Actes du Congrès International de Philosophie Scientifique* 4 (1936): 18 and 23.

What sets "Bewährung" apart from a simple mystical bridge between the human and eternity (and makes it relevant today) is the negativity of the mechanism of representation at work in the relationship that "Bewährung" posits between the finite and infinite. As Leora Batnitzky writes, representation takes on a special meaning for Rosenzweig, signifying not a mode of presentation, but rather the act of standing-in-for, in the sense of the German *Vertreter* and *vertreten*, "which mean 'representative' and 'to represent' in *a political and ethical sense*."[24] Representation plays a key role in the larger theological claim of *The Star of Redemption*, which is that Christian and Jewish liturgical practice "verifies" the truth of God by representing in finite experience (human work in the world) the eternity of redemption (the Kingdom of God). As finite (experiential) and eternal (circular), these yearly liturgical forms "represent the redeemed supra-world to knowledge," but, as Rosenzweig cautions, "knowledge only recognizes them; it does not see beyond them."[25] Here we see the negativity of representation, a moment of ontological non-identity, in which one thing may stand in and act in place of another, but will never be it.

"Bewährung" allows for knowledge to be empirical and experiential, but this moment of non-identity sets limits to the epistemological claims of empiricism that avoid a false postulate of totality, as in positivism. "Verification [*Bewährung*] takes place in that which is most one's own, in the individual life" (e. g., participating in the liturgical cycles), *The Star of Redemption* claims, but where the "whole" truth cannot itself become the matter of human experience, it "can be seen [*geschaut*]. Not experienced: for this we have recognized, that the highest only falls to humans' share when it becomes part. But seen."[26] Intimately tied to the topic of idolatry, this passage makes an important distinction: while humans never experience the Absolute, we "see" the Absolute as represented in the religious experience of liturgy.[27] We can have representatives of the Absolute, but knowledge of the Absolute in any representative becomes false once we take a representation for that which it represents. Beyond its theological stakes, "Bewährung" opens up the possibility of a form of knowledge that is empirical and metaphysical at the same time, in which experience is a form of knowing that becomes knowledge only when set into a relationship with a claim to the Absolute that transcends the parameters of human finitude.

---

24 Leora Batnitzky, *Idolatry and Representation: The Philosophy of Franz Rosenzweig Reconsidered* (Princeton: Princeton University Press, 2000), 29.
25 Rosenzweig, *The Star of Redemption*, 312. [translation modified]
26 Rosenzweig, 417. [translation modified]
27 For more on Rosenzweig's thinking on idolatry, see Batnitzky, *Idolatry and Representation*, here, 12.

The representative relationship between the empirical and the metaphysical proposed by "Bewährung" broadens the epistemological horizons in which we can think about the so-called positive knowledge produced by digital work. My goal here, I remind readers, is not to build a strict analogy between "Bewährung" and the digital humanities—that the activities of a digital archivist, as important as they are, represent some kind of divine Absolute. Instead, consider a visualization of the correspondence networks from Rosenzweig's partial archive deposited at the University of Kassel, which I created from an archival finding aid and published in 2015. The image shows the interconnections of approximately one thousand letters sent primarily to and from Rosenzweig and his family (e. g., Edith Rosenzweig, Adele and Georg Rosenzweig) and intellectual interlocutors (his cousins, Hans and Rudolf Ehrenberg). As correspondences were an important site of intellectual exchange for Rosenzweig, visualizing these networks offers scholars of Rosenzweig insight into how he shaped interwar debates on translation theory (as in the letters between Ernst Simon and Siegfried Kracauer) and renders legible the presence in his archive of voices marginalized in his collected works and research into his thought (especially those of his female correspondents, such as Margarete Susman).[28] The data from the Kassel archive and its visualization, which following sections expand with further and updated data from Rosenzweig holdings, presents to scholars an image (a representative, to use Rosenzweig's term) of the social structure of German Jewish personal and intellectual life surrounding Rosenzweig.

And yet, in terms of "Bewährung," this image as a "representative" contains and exhibits the negative dimension of representation. For instance, it flattens the temporality of hundreds of letters, which were exchanged over the course of century; it lacks the content of the letters; and it obscures the fact that the correspondences housed in Kassel are only a part of a complete archive of Rosenzweig's extant work. Beyond the structures of Rosenzweig's correspondence networks, the visualization offers such negative markers of the discontinuities in Rosenzweig's diasporic archive and the multi-generational attempt, which began during his lifetime, to preserve his philosophical and theological legacy.[29]

---

[28] For instance, Ernst Simon and Edith Rosenzweig jointly published Rosenzweig's letters in 1935, six years after his death, as Franz Rosenzweig, *Briefe*, ed. Ernst Simon and Edith Rosenzweig (Berlin: Schocken Verlag, 1935).

[29] One of the first moments of archival preservation was that of Rosenzweig's mother, Adele Rosenzweig, who, as researchers believe, made a 444-page typescript of her son's letters home during World War I (between August 1914 and July 1917). Wolfgang D. Herzfeld, "Einleitung," in *Feldpostbriefe: Die Korrespondenz mit den Eltern*, ed. Wolfgang D. Herzfeld (Freiburg: Verlag Karl Alber, 2013), 26–27.

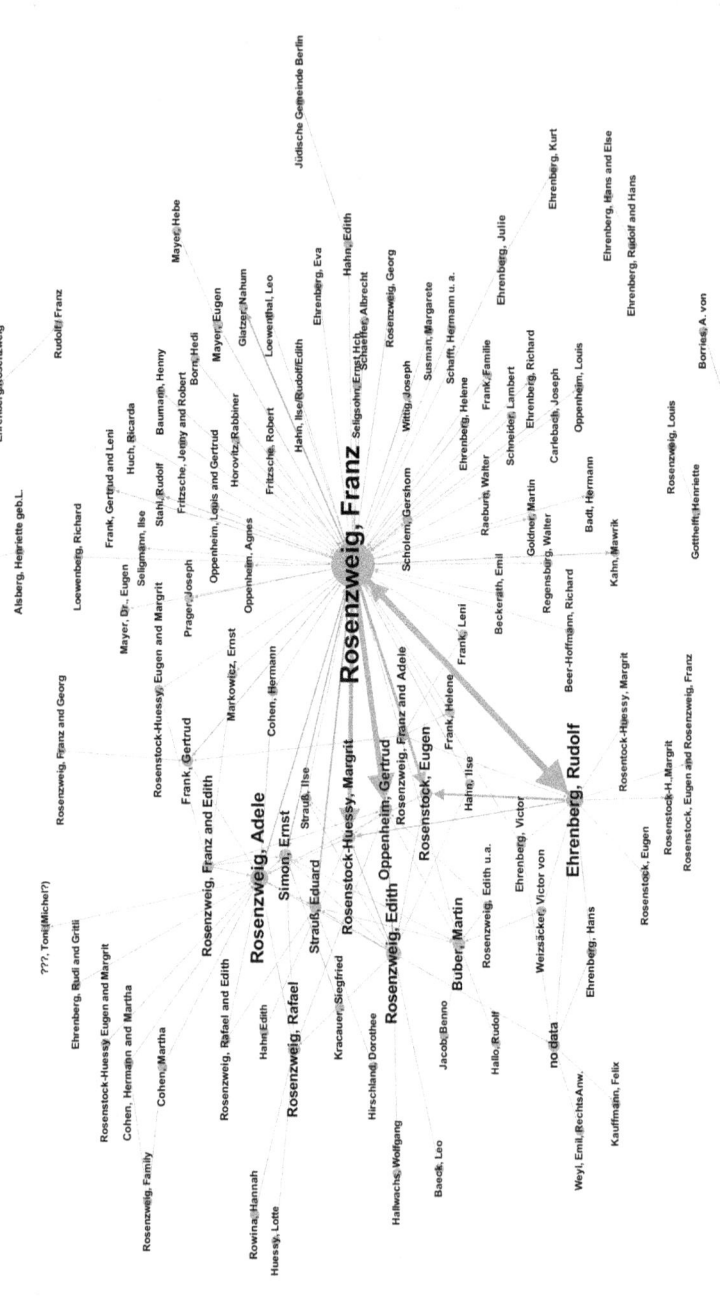

Figure 1: Visualization of the Kassel metadata via PDF finding aid.

Developing strategies to interpret this negativity would expand on what Johanna Drucker has called for as a "visual epistemology" appropriate for humanities data.[30] The visualization of Rosenzweig's archive thus not only produces positive knowledge to guide future research into Rosenzweig's work, but also, through its own limitations, hints at the theoretical—indeed, transcendental—preconditions that make knowledge of such an archive possible.

2 Temporality

The procedural nature of liturgy implies that one of the transcendental preconditions of the knowledge produced by "Bewährung" is temporality: our actions "verify" beliefs in our time and in the absolute course of time. Here, transcendental does not denote an ecstatic, esoteric, or, even, aesthetic mode by which humans can escape the limitations of finitude. Recall, instead, the distinction that Kant draws between "transcendent" and "transcendental": where transcendent objects exceed the possibilities of experience, "transcendental" signifies "our mode of cognition of objects insofar as this is to be possible *a priori*."[31] Transcendental principles are the conditions of possibility that allow us to have knowledge of objects. At points, the theoretical language of the transcendental, as with that of Rosenzweig's theology, seems at odds with the digital humanities and research enabled by archival and library data.[32] Nonetheless, the political and ethical claims of the digital humanities, which have become central to its critical vocation, raise a number of salient questions about the conditions of knowledge and action in the digital age, such as how we are to understand and evaluate projects, like that of mapping Rosenzweig's correspondence networks, which exceed the limits of any individual researcher.[33] As Rosenzweig's

---

30 Johanna Drucker, *Graphesis: Visual Forms of Knowledge Production* (Cambridge: Harvard University Press, 2014), 6.
31 Immanuel Kant, *Critique of Pure Reason*, trans. Paul Guyer and Allen W. Wood (Cambridge: Cambridge University Press, 1999), 149.
32 On this dynamic between digital humanities and theory, see the contributions to *Journal of Digital Humanities*, special issue on theory, especially: Natalia Cecire, "Introduction: Theory and the Virtues of Digital Humanities," *Journal of Digital Humanities* 1, no. 1 (Winter 2011), http://journalofdigitalhumanities.org/1-1/introduction-theory-and-the-virtues-of-digital-humanities-by-natalia-cecire/.
33 For instance, Roopika Risam has forcefully shown that digital humanities (and, in particular, what she explores as postcolonial digital humanities) can "remake the worlds instantiated in the digital cultural record through politically, ethically, and social justice-minded approaches," *New*

response to a similar set of epistemological concerns, "Bewährung" suggests that a more complicated notion of temporality than simply that of an empty continuum, stretching from past to future, conditions the possibility of knowledge in the digital humanities.

One of Rosenzweig's most lucid explanations of the temporal dimension of "Bewährung" occurs in his brief correspondence with Siegfried Kracauer, a German Jewish journalist and later film theorist. Kracauer was deeply skeptical of the entwinement of philosophy and theology that runs throughout *The Star of Redemption* and Rosenzweig's thought.[34] Rosenzweig's letter from March 1923 thus tries to convince Kracauer of the possibility that a system of belief can serve as a means of connecting the individual with the Absolute:

> There is a way whereby an epoch, an -ism, or something similar can become absolute. But it eludes knowledge by proof or demonstration [...]; for its object is neither rational nor "irrational," but rather much simpler: not yet there at all. It's a question of a becoming-absolute, not of a being-absolute, a question of the one by the grace of the other; in a certain sense, a being-absolute by partial payments. It depends on whether the installments are paid on time—historically or, respectively, personally on time. Hence, logically (new-logically) speaking: it depends not on proof, but on verification [*nicht auf den Beweis, sondern auf die Bewährung*].[35]

This passage abounds with imagery and terminological distinctions, such as that between "proof" (*Beweis*) and "verification" (*Bewährung*), to which I will return.[36] Its main point, however, is to describe the temporal frame in which "Bewährung" occurs: we produce knowledge in human time as an "epoch" (e.g., the postwar period) or a religious "-ism" (Judaism) participates in an unending (as described in *The Star of Redemption*) process of becoming an Absolute state of existence (the Kingdom of God). Amidst the skepticism and social changes of the early twentieth century, "Bewährung" upheld the possibility of knowledge, even if the "proof" of its absolute validity, in any logical or scientific sense of the word, stands outside of historical time.

Digital Worlds: Postcolonial Digital Humanities in Theory, Praxis, and Pedagogy (Evanston: Northwestern University Press, 2019), 4.
34 See Matthew Handelman, "The Forgotten Conversation. Five Letters from Franz Rosenzweig to Siegfried Kracauer, 1921–1923," *Scientia Poetica* 15 (2011): 234–251.
35 Cited in Stephanie Baumann, "Drei Briefe – Franz Rosenzweig an Siegfried Kracauer," *Zeitschrift für Religions- und Geistesgeschichte* 63, no. 2 (2011): 174–75.
36 For instance, the word "installments" invokes Max Weber's sociological use of "Bewährung" in his analyses of Protestantism, Max Weber, *The Protestant Ethic and the "Spirit" of Capitalism and Other Writings*, trans. Peter Baehr and Grodon C. Wells (New York: Penguin, 2002), 208.

As the letter hints, the temporalities that condition the knowledge proper to "Bewährung" are really three different scales of time: the "personal" dimension of time, as in the work of an individual's lifetime, the "historical" dimension, as in the lifespan of epochs, and the Absolute dimension of time, as in the end of human time and beginning of the messianic age on earth. In contrast to a proof that flattens time by "demonstrating" the validity of a statement once and for all ("being-absolute"), "Bewährung" designates a form of knowledge that accrues over time as individuals ("personal") and groups ("historical") "invest" in it over the absolute course of time. Here, we again see the productive negativity of the concept of "Bewährung," as knowledge that "becomes absolute" through time, but is a perpetual "not yet there" Absolute. One way to think about the first two temporalities is from the viewpoint of an individual engaged in such process-based knowledge, such as, to borrow an example from Friedrich Hölderlin, the poet who also must "bear the momentarily incomplete" in the process of writing.[37] For Hölderlin, who was an important figure in Rosenzweig's work and intellectual biography, the creative mind remains in the moment to moment succession of writing the poem, while neither forgetting nor prematurely declaring the totality of its finished state.[38] The concept of "Bewährung" adds a third temporal dimension: messianic time, which serves as a vanishing point that orients personal time away from the dangers of subjectivism (the view that my perspective is the Absolute) and relativism (that the Absolute is relative to a historical period). In contrast to knowledge that we "prove" to be eternally true, the process-based knowledge of "Bewährung" indicates that open-ended, long-term projects in the digital humanities may operate in distinct yet interrelated temporalities, such as those of individuals, groups, and a regulative totality akin to Rosenzweig's Absolute.

Reading on all three temporal levels gives form to the knowledge offered by the images of Rosenzweig's archive, but it also helps such digital work avoid the naivety of positivism. To be sure, there is an indirect resemblance between the actions of the believer in "Bewährung" and the critical work involved in creating

---

37 Friedrich Hölderlin, "Reflection," in *Friedrich Hölderlin: Essays and Letters on Theory*, trans. Thomas Pfau (Albany: SUNY Press, 1988), 46.
38 On Hölderlin's theory of poetry, see the work of Hannah Eldridge, whom I have to thank for the reference; Hannah Vandegrift Eldridge, *Lyric Orientations: Hölderlin, Rilke, and the Poetics of Community* (Ithaca: Cornell University Press, 2016), chap. 2. Hölderlin was one of the three suspected collaborators on the text "The Oldest System-Program of German Idealism," which Rosenzweig found in 1914 in the Prussian State Library and published in 1917, giving the text its title. On the role of German Idealism and the "Oldest System-Program of German Idealism," see Pollock, *Franz Rosenzweig and the Systematic Task of Philosophy*, chap. 1.

and updating such a project.³⁹ But consider the product of a second iteration of visualizing Rosenzweig's archive, which includes updated metadata from the University of Kassel as well as the metadata of Rosenzweig's correspondences deposited at Vanderbilt University's Divinity Library, the Leo Baeck Institute (New York), and the German Literary Archive (Deutsches Literaturarchiv, Marbach am Neckar).⁴⁰ The entangled network surrounding the ego-node (Rosenzweig) indicates a deeper complexity to the structure of intellectual and personal exchange that informed Rosenzweig's thought, only the surface of which extant literature and archival publications scratch. Similar to Klein's "images of absence," we can think of these visualizations as positive images of erasure, which sketches the outlines of a German Jewish community disrupted by the rise of National Socialism and the exile of its members, Rosenzweig's family included.⁴¹

However, the network posited by these images raises the problem indicated in the Marcuse quote with which I began this article. For Marcuse, to take these data, the "matters of fact" as presented by such visualizations as a final authority, as in positivism, collapses the individual and historical levels of time with that of the messianic, presenting its image as final and fixed. It posits images

---

39 The iterative nature of digital humanities is a foundational trope, see Burdick et al., *Digital_Humanities*, 21.

40 These images include metadata from the partial archive at the University of Kassel; "Franz Rosenzweig," n.d., https://www.uni-kassel.de/ub/landesbibliothek/sondersammlungen/nachlaesse/rosenzweig. I have included the names of correspondents and number of letters at the Leo Baeck Institute in New York, but excluded those between Rosenzweig and his parents; "Collection: Franz Rosenzweig Collection," n.d., https://archives.cjh.org//repositories/5/resources/11012. I have incorporated correspondent names and numbers of letters, such as Rosenzweig's letters to Kracauer, from the Deutsches Literaturarchiv and those at the Glatzer Collection at Vanderbilt University; "Franz Rosenzweig Papers | Collection Guides," n.d., https://collections.library.vanderbilt.edu/repositories/2/archival_objects/217531. Due to the lack of available metadata at the time of writing, I have not included Rosenzweig's letters held at Dartmouth College and the National Library of Israel.

41 Rosenzweig's wife, Edith, and son, Rafael, immigrated to Palestine in 1938, while others, such as Kracauer and Rosenstock, emigrated to the United States and others, such as Leo Baeck, to England; on Kracauer's exile, see Johannes von Moltke, *The Curious Humanist: Siegfried Kracauer in America* (Berkeley: University of California Press, 2016). On Edith and Rafel's exile (and the fate of Rosenzweig's personal library), see Rafael Rosenzweig, "Augenblicke," in *Vergegenwärtigungen des zerstörten jüdischen Erbes: Franz-Rosenzweig-Gastvorlesungen Kassel 1987–1998*, ed. Wolfdietrich Schmied-Kowarzik (Kassel: Kassel University Press, 1997), 319–32; Norbert Waszek, *Rosenzweigs Bibliothek: Der Katalog des Jahres 1939 mit einem Bericht über den derzeitigen Zustand in der tunesischen Nationalbibliothek* (Freiburg: Verlag Karl Alber, 2017), 11. See also Julia Schneidawind, "A Diaspora of Books – Franz Rosenzweig's Library in Tunis," Jewish Culture and History 22, no. 2 (2021): 140–53.

A Messianic Theory of Digital Knowledge — 45

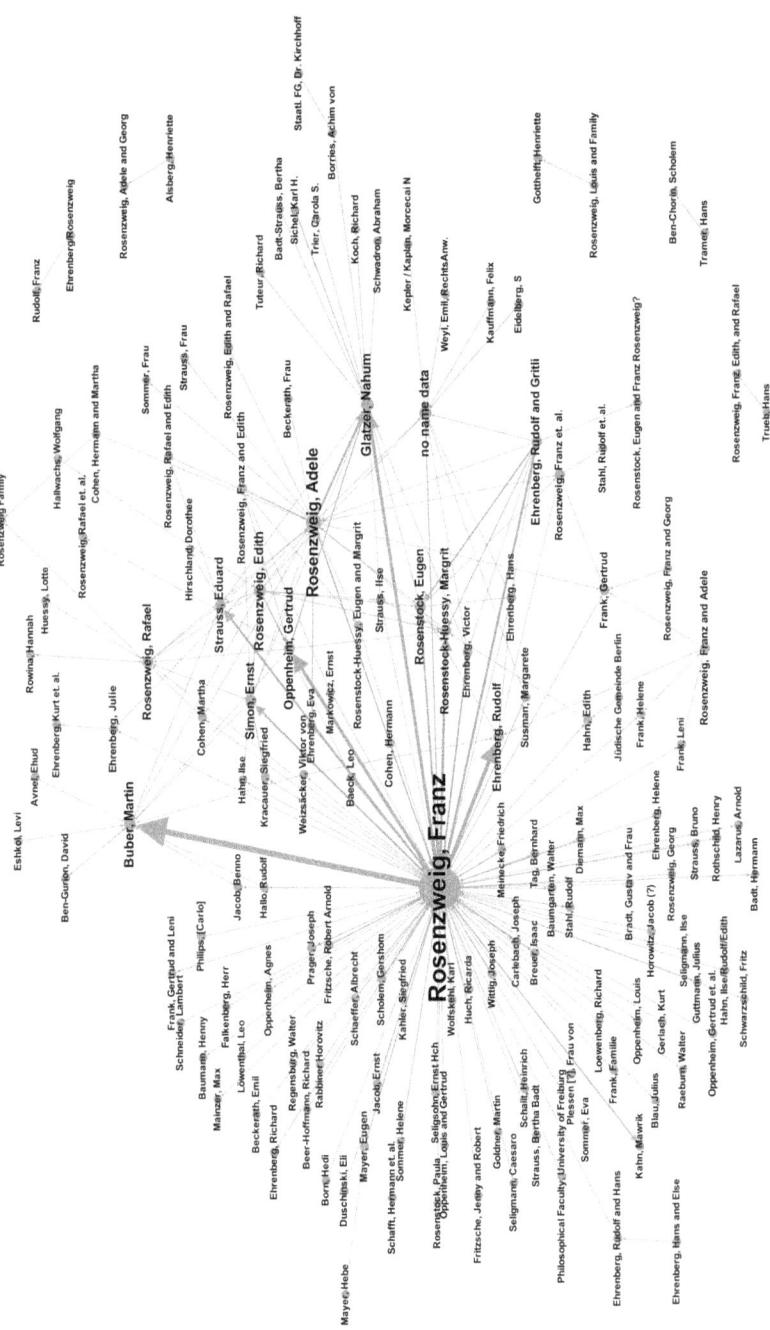

Figure 2: Refined Kassel metadata expanded to include metadata from the Leo Baeck Institute, Vanderbilt, and DLA.

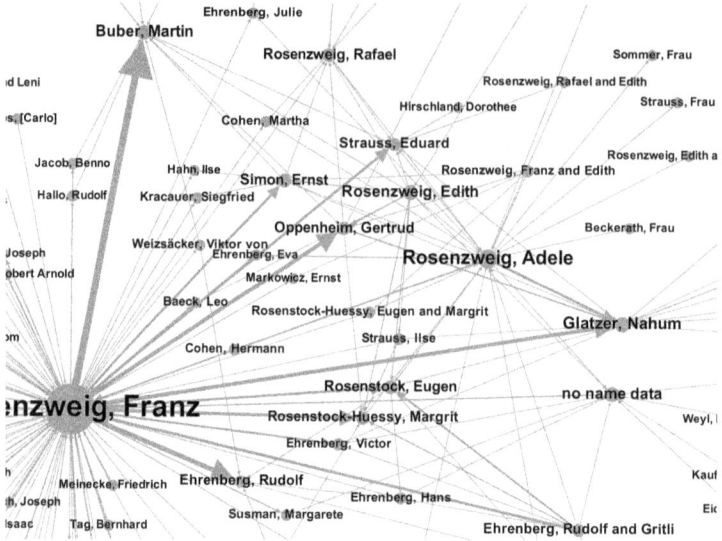

Figure 3: Close up of connections surrounding Rosenzweig.

of Rosenzweig's archive, without asking how the experience of exile and its interruption of the archival record shaped these images or imagining what they may have looked like without the disruptions of World War II. Considered in the light of "Bewährung," the contrast between initial and revised visualizations of Rosenzweig's archive shows something similar: while we improve on the breadth and accuracy of their representations and even our method of representing itself, there remains a moment of negativity in the temporal distance between our incomplete and finite work on Rosenzweig's legacy and the complete (messianic?) reconstruction of his archive.

Coming to interpretative terms with this negativity is a matter of locating and reading the discontinuities in the visualization and the moments at which the computational manipulation of metadata falters and fails. As mentioned in the first section, this image of Rosenzweig's archive flattens the temporality of the metadata and produces an overview of a social network at the cost of the granularity of data. But, at the same time, it also hints at the discontinuities and gaps in the archive as Rosenzweig's correspondence network prematurely terminates at the nodes of family, friends, and other interlocutors. For instance, the node of the conservative historian, Siegfried A. Kaehler, appears as a terminus, despite Kaehler's own correspondences with figures significant to Rosenzweig, such as Margrit and Eugen Rosenstock.[42] Moreover, we see a number of diodes discontinuous with the rest of the network, indicating the letters between Hans Tramer, the first chairman of the Leo Baeck Institute, and the historian Schalom Ben-Chorin in the Rosenzweig subset of the Nahum N. Glatzer Collection at Vanderbilt University, which represent the postwar preservation of German Jewish culture. As much as the visualizations provide positive images of erasure, a shadow of German Jewish intellectual life before war and in exile, their discontinuities and endpoints reveal not the "momentarily," but rather the perpetually "incomplete" state of any reconstruction of Rosenzweig's archive. These signs of non-totality are appeals to readers to take note, as many digital humanists put it, of the "future-oriented" nature of digital work and to put these particular images into dialog with the expansive temporal dimensions that they invoke: the work of generations of scholars in building Rosenzweig's archive and the negative moment of history itself.[43] In this sense, to understand the knowledge produced by these images would mean formulating an epistemology that takes account of the open-ended temporal dimensions involved in working with library and archival data—an idea that Rosenzweig's letter to Kracauer hints at through its epistemological distinction between "proof" (*Beweis*) and "verification" (*Bewährung*).

3 Epistemology

The foundational epistemological problem addressed by "Bewährung" is the absence of a substantiation by which we recognize knowledge as valid, in as much as such substantiation lies beyond the parameters of finite experience. In mathematics and logic, the standard method of demonstrating the validity of a statement is "proof" (*Beweis*): to prove a claim, in mathematical debates of Rosenzweig's time, was to be able to determine its validity (or invalidity) through a finite number of logical steps.[44] (In the 1930s, it was by working through similar

---

[42] In "Nachlass Siegfried A. Kaehler," n.d., http://hans.sub.uni-goettingen.de/nachlaesse/Kaehler_Siegfried_August.pdf.
[43] See Matthew Kirschenbaum, "Digital Humanities As/Is a Tactical Term," in *Debates in the Digital Humanities*, ed. Matthew K. Gold (Minneapolis: University of Minnesota Press, 2012), 416; Bethany Nowviskie, "Reconstitute the World," *Bethany Nowviskie* (blog), June 12, 2018, http://nowviskie.org/2018/reconstitute-the-world/.
[44] See Rudolf Eisler, *Handwörterbuch der Philosophie*, 2nd ed., ed. Richard Müller-Friedenfels (Berlin: Mittler, 1922), 98. On the question of the possibility of a proof's finitude, see George Dys-

ideas that Alan Turing described the idea of a so-called Turing machine: a mathematical model of computation, which set the stage for digital computers.[45]) Proof requires that individuals, mathematicians and scientists, show that a statement, to use Rosenzweig's terms, "is Absolute" in the finitude of their existence or to provide empirical evidence that definitively upholds their claims. But what about forms of knowledge for which the evidence cannot be the matter of finite experience—such as the existence of God—or for which a substantiation reaches beyond the temporal limits of an individual's and generation's lifespan—such as social change that combats racism? Are we to demote them, as in positivism, from the ranks of knowledge? "Bewährung," which Rosenzweig calls "the true proof [*der wahre Beweis*]," proposes an answer to these questions by turning proof inside out: instead of objects needing to be proved, it makes knowledge depend on the objectivity of our actions.[46] Mediating between scientific, mathematical, and religious forms of knowledge, "Bewährung" presents an epistemology that includes provable knowledge and knowledge which lacks proof, such as human activity, without totalizing the one or the other.

While the term started out as a link between believer and "the 'whole' truth" in *The Star of Redemption*, "Bewährung" signals what an epistemological paradigm shift, with relevance to the status of knowledge in the digital humanities, may ultimately look like. Rosenzweig's essay, "The New Thinking" (1925), explicitly calls "Bewährung" a "messianic theory of knowledge" (*messianische Erkenntnistheorie*), which is "messianic" in that it defers the substantiation of knowledge beyond finite, human experience. Accordingly:

> truth ceases to be what "is" true and becomes that which [wants to be] *verified* as true. The concept of the verification of truth becomes the basic concept of this new epistemology, which takes the place of the old epistemology's non-contradiction theory and object theory, and introduces, instead of the old static concept of objectivity, a dynamic concept. The hopelessly static truths, like those of mathematics, which were made into the point of departure by the old epistemology, without ever getting beyond this point of departure, are to be conceived from this perspective as the—lower—limiting case, as rest is conceived as the limiting case of motion, while the higher and highest truths are only capable of being grasped as truths from this perspective, instead of having to be relabeled as fictions, postulates, and needs. From those most unimportant truths of the type "two times two is four," on which people easily agree, with no other expense than a little bit of brainpower—for the

---

on's accessible discussion in George Dyson, *Turing's Cathedral: The Origins of the Digital Universe* (New York: Vintage, 2012), 246–49.

45 See Dyson, *Turing's Cathedral*, 247–48.

46 Franz Rosenzweig, *Understanding the Sick and the Healthy: A View of World, Man, and God*, trans. Nahum Norbert Glatzer (Cambridge: Harvard University Press, 1999), 36. [translation modified]

multiplication table a little less, for the theory of relativity a little more—the way leads over those truths, for which a person is willing to pay, over to those, which a person cannot verify in any other way than with the sacrifice of his life, and finally to those whose truth can be verified only by the commitment of the lives of all generations.[47]

This passage asks the reader to reconsider the relationship between objects and their ability to be knowledge. In the first line, the passage rejects the idea that "truth" (akin to the Absolute in the Kracauer letter) can be considered to be a property of an object (for example: "this sentence *is* true"). Instead, again drawing attention to human activity through the use of the passive, it claims that "truth" *needs* the action of individuals ("sacrifice" and "commitment") to *make* it true ("this statement *wants* to be verified *by* someone"). It is not that an object *is* true, but rather that I, as an acting individual, and my actions as objects in the world (e.g., partaking in liturgical cycles) *make* themselves true in relation to the Absolute. Amidst the rising hegemony of scientific rationality, "Bewährung" gave voice to an alternative, future-oriented epistemology that weighs knowledge according not to its eternal validity, but rather to the "commitments" that we make to it.

The concept of "Bewährung" in Rosenzweig's "messianic theory of knowledge" holds relevance for digital work in that it proposes a "dynamic" spectrum of knowledge production that ranges from science and mathematics to religion and ethical action, without rejecting the one or the other. By making human action the "objective" epistemological standard, the passage here redefines the "perspective" from which we view knowledge. On the one hand, we can think of the "static" knowledge of mathematics as epistemologically trivial—or, in Rosenzweig's words, "unimportant"—precisely because it can be proved to be irrefutable and eternal.[48] On the other hand, the open-ended processes of experience, such as work dedicated to a group or community, become the "higher" case of knowledge, because, while they lack a demonstrable proof, people are nonetheless willing to "pay" or "sacrifice their lives" for them. For Rosenzweig, then, knowledge is empirical and "objective" to the extent that we, from individuals to all generations, live out this knowledge in the world, across individuals

---

[47] Franz Rosenzweig, "The New Thinking," in *Philosophical and Theological Writings*, trans. Paul Franks and Michael Morgan (Indianapolis: Hackett, 2000), 135–36.

[48] By trivial, I mean that Rosenzweig presents a view of mathematics that borders on the notion that mathematics is one big tautology: all mathematical knowledge unfolds logically and analytically (e.g., without any empirical input) out of itself, meaning that it is only a matter of logical steps that lead from the "multiplication tables" to the "theory of relativity." On the origins of this viewpoint, see Handelman, *Mathematical Imagination*, chap. 2.

and generations. Beyond Rosenzweig's rhetoric, we see a final productive moment of negativity in "Bewährung" here: while few would risk their money (let alone lives) to wager that 2 + 2 = 4, the deeper, protean dimension of knowledge lies in ideas to which people freely dedicate their lives despite lacking confirmation of their validity. In terms of process-based and open-ended knowledge in the digital humanities, "Bewährung" suggests a shift in emphasis from discussions over the novelty and eternal validity of digital work to an epistemic paradigm that values knowledge, such as that provided by the metadata of Rosenzweig's archive, both for what it does in the world and in the context of the larger ethical, political, and epistemological goals in which it works.

We see these dynamics in interactions between the efforts of librarians, archivists, and researchers and the metadata and visualizations of Rosenzweig's archive, both of which work within the framework of ongoing research into Rosenzweig's life and work and German Jewish cultural and intellectual history. Especially as libraries and archives make archival finding aids available online and increase access to their metadata and materials, these data present us with the horizon of Rosenzweig's material record, codetermining, as researchers adjust their research practices in the digital age, the direction of archival research.[49] As researchers compile ever more complex data about Rosenzweig's archive—connecting it to, for instance, metadata from Kracauer's and Susman's archives—these data and visualizations also reframe our picture of Rosenzweig's intellectual milieu and of German Jewish social life in general.[50] With the increased number of data points, this network draws attention to the centrality of a few specific nodes as interconnections of both archival holdings and distinct social groups in prewar Germany. By consciously designing the data to reflect a more inclusive view of German Jewish intellectual history, the image also serves as the site in which researchers can call attention to and begin investigation into underrepresented figures, such as Margarete Susman. We see close-up that Susman served as a significant actor in this intellectual milieu, connecting figures close to the Frankfurt School (e.g., Kracauer and Bloch) with members of the Jewish cultural renewal movement (e.g., Rosenzweig and Buber). While Susman moved away from Frankfurt in 1921 (and to a place, Bad Säckingen, which lies

---

49 See Jonathan Hess's reflections on the changes that massive digitization brings to German Jewish Studies, in "Studying Print Culture in the Digital Age," *The Leo Baeck Institute Yearbook* 54 (2009): 33–36.

50 I take this constellation of thinkers as a central component of Weimar-era Jewish intellectual life in Germany; see my article "The Forgotten Conversation" and Harry T. Craver, *Reluctant Skeptic: Siegfried Kracauer and the Crises of Weimar Culture* (New York: Berghahn, 2017). Data for these archives can be found at "Kalliope Verbund," n.d., https://kalliope-verbund.info/.

literally on the margins of Germany) to care for her ailing child, these images help Susman reclaim her centrality in the Weimar-era Jewish intellectual networks.[51] These visualizations—importantly—help us create a more inclusive picture of German Jewish intellectual history. But, fixed into a positive image, they risk falling prey to the idea that improvements in technological modes of representation can overcome the processes of marginalization, oppression, and erasure of the past and, in the end, vanquish them from our modes of representation in the future.

As it defers the final substantiation of knowledge beyond finite experience, "Bewährung" reminds digital humanists that paying attention to the negativity that inheres in the production of knowledge provides a means to avoid such a methodological positivism. Part of this task lies, as digital humanists such as Roopika Risam and Miriam Posner explain, in reworking technologies so that they do not recapitulate colonial, patriarchal, and Eurocentric systems of knowledge and power.[52] Another part, "Bewähung" suggests, lies in reading the limitations—the lack of context and the formality of the network—of visualizing Rosenzweig's archive as a marker of negativity in our methods, both historical and digital. This negativity—a trade-off between a view of social interconnections for content—abounds in these visualizations, if not the digital humanities as a whole, indicating the need for hybrid epistemologies that would read Rosenzweig's thought in terms of both context and structure. Such an epistemology would draw, in part, on the methods of intellectual history, as employed in this article: contextualizing ideas in their specific historical time and place, such as the role of mysticism and the infinite in modernity, and closely reading their development over time. At the same time, it would conceptualize intellectual discourse as a network of ideas that do not develop so much as they circulate (such as the infinite after World War I) and take on conceptual forms (such as "Bewährung") as they move and evolve between individuals.[53] As "Bewährung" mediates between mathematical and religious knowledge, such an epistemology

---

51 See Margarete Susman, *Ich habe viele Leben gelebt* (Stuttgart: Deutsche Verlags-Anstalt, 1964); Ingrid Belke, "Siegfried Kracauer: Geschichte einer Begegnung," in *Grenzgänge zwischen Dichtung, Philosophie und Kulturkritik: Über Margarete Susman*, ed. Anke Gilleir and Barbara Hahn (Göttingen: Wallstein, 2012), 35–61.
52 See Risam, *New Digital Worlds*, 17. Miriam Posner, "What's Next: The Radical, Unrealized Potential of Digital Humanities," in *Debates in the Digital Humanities 2016*, ed. Matthew K. Gold and Lauren F. Klein (Minneapolis: University of Minnesota Press, 2016), 35.
53 This idea resonates with Barbara Hahn's proposal of a "network of relations or perhaps a 'weave'" as a way to represent what remains legible of Jewish women writers' contribution to German modernity; see *The Jewess Pallas Athena: This Too a Theory of Modernity*, trans. James McFarland (Princeton: Princeton University Press, 2005), 13.

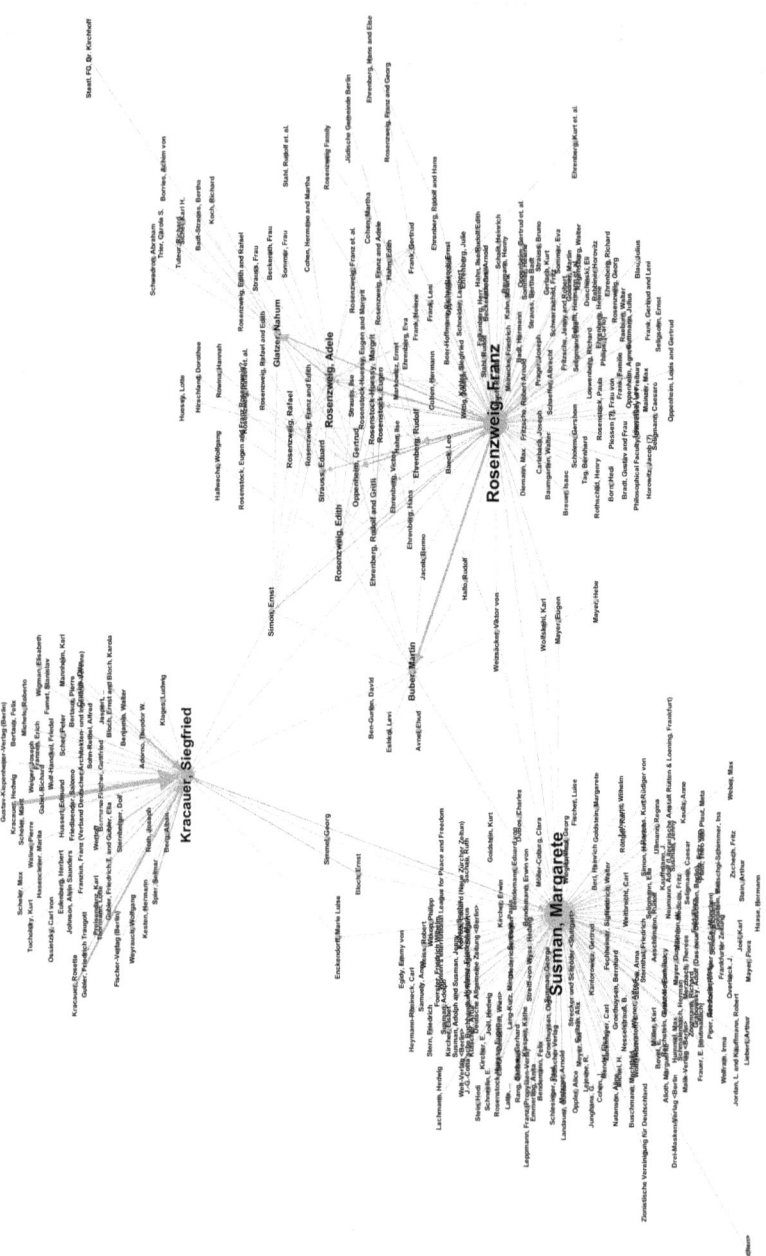

Figure 4: Visualization of Rosenzweig, Kracauer, and Susman metadata.

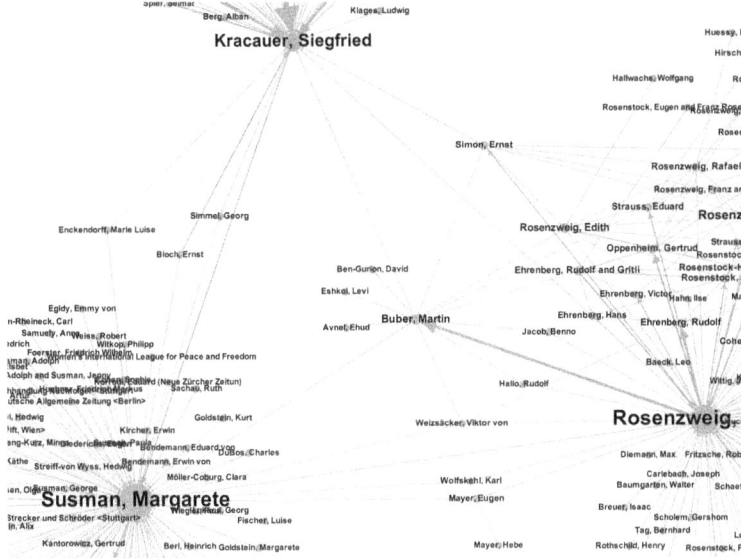

Figure 5: Close up of interconnections among Rosenzweig, Kracauer, and Susman.

would draw on both technical-scientific and close reading forms of knowledge, taking its own multi-disciplinarity as a representative of the not-yet-totality of our knowledge of both Rosenzweig and German Jewish intellectual life in the twentieth century.

4 Conclusion: Rosenzweig in/and the Digital Age

To return to the warning from Herbert Marcuse at the start of this article, the concept of "Bewährung" in Franz Rosenzweig's philosophy helps contemporary scholars come to terms with not only the potential but also the positivistic pitfalls of library and archival data and, more generally, the digital humanities. As seen in the visualizations of the correspondences that make up Rosenzweig's archive, library and archival data provides "positive" images of Rosenzweig's intellectual milieu and a partial visual reconstruction of the intellectual exchange that made up German Jewish life before National Socialism and characterized its continuation in exile. Along with drawing attention to underexplored intellectual voices in the network, the metadata of these archives and their visualization raise the possibility—and it would take the efforts of generations to achieve—of establishing an online, cross-institutional repository of Rosenzweig's archival holdings, including a database of extant archival materials, copies of relevant texts in the public domain, and even digitizations of these materials.[54] This online archive would include materials discussed here, but also Rosenzweig's manuscripts and holdings from institutions with smaller Rosenzweig collections, which would make these resources accessible to students and scholars while allowing institutions to retain their holdings. The aim of this imagined archive taps into the progressive and emancipatory goals of digital work in the humanities: it promises to overcome the limits of the diaspora of archival materials and institutional politics, bringing back together, at least virtually, that which persecution, exile, and war broke apart.

In converse, Rosenzweig's concept of "Bewährung" and its associated "messianic theory of knowledge" provide strategies to avoid the political and ethical dangers of positivism involved with working with the library and archival data that make up Rosenzweig's archive—such as the idea of a unified Rosenzweig archive. Both the positivistic impulse to take the empirically given, the "data," as the totality of what is and the hope that scientific-technological methods may help compensate for the errors of the past are what make the visualizations of Rosenzweig's archive and the imagination of a unified Rosenzweig archive so seductive. They also underpin much of the writing on big data and business analytics on which the digital humanities often draws. Take, for instance, the idea that, as Kenneth Cukier and Viktor Mayer-Schönberger write, sampling in scientific experiments will come to an end as we reach an era in which sample sizes are "n = *all*."[55] As the term "n = all" parallels Rosenzweig's own investigation of the fate of "the All" in philosophy, the link that "Bewährung" forges between finitude and totality tempers positivism by reminding us of the irreducible metaphysical and theological dimensions of these claims—if not, as Clifford Anderson writes, the digital humanities as a whole.[56] The suppressed metaphysics in

---

[54] This iterative approach has been the model by which Rosenzweig's materials have appeared in print, from the first publication of his letters before World War II to their postwar expansion and republication in Franz Rosenzweig, *Der Mensch und sein Werk: Briefe und Tagebücher*, ed. Rachel Rosenzweig, Edith Rosenzweig-Scheinmann, and Bernhard Casper, 2 vols. (The Hauge: Martinus Nijhoff, 1979). Recent archival publications include Rosenzweig's wartime letters to his parents, in Franz Rosenzweig, *Feldpostbriefe: Die Korrespondenz mit den Eltern (1914–1917)*, ed. Wolfgang D Herzfeld (Freiburg: K. Alber, 2013).
[55] Viktor Mayer-Schönberger and Kenneth Cukier, *Big Data: A Revolution That Will Transform How We Live, Work, and Think* (Boston: Houghton Mifflin Harcourt, 2013), 26–31. See also Russell Walker, *From Big Data to Big Profits: Success with Data and Analytics* (Oxford: Oxford University Press, 2015), 17–19.
[56] Clifford Anderson, "Digital Humanities and the Future of Theology," *Cursor_* 1: Neuland (July 24, 2018), https://cursor.pubpub.org/pub/anderson-digitalhumanities-2018.

the program of logical positivism was, after all, one of the criticisms that Horkheimer and Adorno made of the Vienna Circle, paving the way for the dialectic of enlightenment.[57]

Perhaps the solution is thus a theory of digital knowledge that would take account of the empirical and metaphysical elements of the digital, as it works in the service of ethics as well as rearranges the horizon of what the term ethics means. This is not to say that the future of digital humanities lies in a return to metaphysics. Rather, it means that the digital humanities stand to learn something from the practical and theoretical questions raised by theology and the concept of "Bewährung," in as much as all three are deeply concerned with questions of representation and temporality, epistemology and ethics. And, ultimately, it means that thinking through how theoretical claims shape our data and how data reshape our theoretical claims will allow us to come to terms with the metaphysical and, indeed, messianic element that has always been a part of any critical theory of digital knowledge.

---

[57] This is the main point of Horkheimer's 1937 essay, "The Latest Attack on Metaphysics," in *Critical Theory: Selected Essays*, trans. Matthew J. O'Connell (New York: Continuum, 2002), 182–84.

Jeri E. Wieringa
Mining Eschatology in Seventh-day Adventist Periodicals

"Move fast and break things." Once the internal motto of Facebook, this approach to the creation of new technologies has shaped cultural patterns around software and the internet, placing a premium on disruption, rapid development, and novelty. Within the digital humanities, much of the early rhetoric around building and experimentation echoed the "build first, ask questions later" ethos of tech communities. As computational methods have continued to develop, the push to stay on the "cutting edge" of new research methods remains strong, with leading figures focusing on applications of deep learning to the textual and visual data of the humanities. While research at the edges of new technologies continues to expand the questions that can be asked, there are open research questions and opportunities all along the lifecycle of digital humanities projects, including data creation and publishing, algorithm development, and preservation. The digital humanities have developed to a point where it is possible and desirable to take a step back and consider what has been accomplished, identify future directions for digital scholarship, and outline the opportunities for collaboration to further the possibilities for and quality of computational research in the humanities.

As an entry point into these questions, I offer my research for *A Gospel of Health and Salvation*, a digital dissertation project in religious history, to illustrate the opportunities and limitations around computational research in history. The digitization of primary source materials has opened new opportunities for research in the humanities, increasing access to historical records and making new types of data available for analysis. As computational research in the humanities has developed, however, the types of data needed for robust analysis have also shifted. Rather than being a burden, I argue that these shifts create opportunities for scholarly collaboration between researchers, librarians, and archivists to support the creation, use, and management of the data sets and algorithms needed for computational analysis of the past. The success of such collaborations requires a shift in attitude from an emphasis on rapid adoption to one of slow cultivation where the complex, labor intensive, and careful work of data creation, algorithm development, and infrastructure building that will support the next generation of computational scholarship can thrive.

1 Building a Text Mining Project in Religious History

In *A Gospel of Health and Salvation* I offer a computational analysis of the periodical literature produced by the Seventh-day Adventist denomination (SDA) between 1849 and 1920. My research is organized around two primary research areas. The first, located within the field of American religious history, explores how beliefs about end-times and constructions of gender interplayed in the development of the religious culture of the SDA during their first seventy years. The transition of the SDA from an emerging religious movement to an established denomination was not a linear progression. Born out of William Miller's teachings regarding end-times and committed to the belief that October 21, 1844 had been correctly identified as the date when the prophecies of the biblical book of Daniel were fulfilled, early Seventh-day Adventists were a people in temporal flux. They understood themselves to be living in the last days while continually wrestling with the continuation of time and the lengthening of their understanding of their temporal position in divine history. This period of instability, both temporally and theologically, led to their development of distinctive beliefs and practices around food, health, and, arguably, gender roles.

The relationship between the end-times beliefs of church members and their shifting cultural ideas about gender are in greater relief in early Seventh-day Adventism because the denomination was under the leadership of Ellen G. White. As a woman prophet and religious leader, White embodied and challenged the complex gender norms of nineteenth-century America. She advocated the sharing of domestic labor between spouses, the wearing of the "American costume," and the need for equitable pay for women denominational workers. She also encouraged women to embrace domestic work as their primary religious calling and was conspicuously silent on questions of women's ordination. The tensions within her writing and her life have made her a challenging figure to understand, particularly in terms of standard accounts of women in radical or emerging religious movements.[1]

---

[1] Scholars who study women in religious movements have frequently used the frameworks of Mary Douglas and Carroll Smith-Rosenberg to explain the prominence of women in leadership during periods of religious revival in terms of the loosening of social structures in the face of economic and social disruption. One of the few scholars to study gender roles in Seventh-day Adventism, Laura Vance, uses this framework, and notes that it is difficult to characterize Ellen White's role in terms of defining gender roles as it is at times progressive and expansive, while at others conservative and restrictive. Mary Douglas, *Purity and Danger: An Analysis of*

The second research area I explore in *A Gospel of Health and Salvation* is methodological, examining the practical and theoretical implications of the application of computational tools to the study of history. Most of the tools used for natural language processing of digital texts, such as named entity recognition and machine learning methods such as topic modeling, were created using texts produced in the twentieth century that consist of technical or academic content. Undertaking computational work as part of historical analysis with digitized sources is still relatively rare and brings with it different challenges and constraints. Through the dissertation, I researched the process of moving from digitized content to historical interpretation, attending to questions of data verification, code reproducibility, and interpretation with complex computational models. In doing so, I raised questions of whether the data and tools currently at hand for computational analysis are sufficient to support robust historical analysis.

To begin a discussion of the future of computational methods in digital history, I will trace my journey from data collection to interpretation of a large collection of the SDA periodical literature. This includes the sourcing and selecting of digital artifacts to work with, the transformation of those into data, the analysis of that data using machine learning, and the interpretation of those results. While somewhat technical at times, these processes constitute a major part of my research in the methodological portions of the dissertation and shape my assessment of the current state and future possibilities for data work in religious studies. They also provide a concrete example of the ways digitized historical artifacts can be used for computational analysis, ways that often go far beyond the initial goals in digitization and publication.

I gathered my data for *A Gospel of Health and Salvation* from the online archives of the Seventh-day Adventist Church.[2] One of the advantages of working with religious history is that there are often networks of volunteers interested in new technologies and in sharing materials with broad audiences. For Seventh-day Adventists, the digitization of their periodical history began in the 1980s with the volunteer work of lay church members with an "interest in computers."[3]

Concepts of Pollution and Taboo (Psychology Press, 2002); Carroll Smith-Rosenberg, *Disorderly Conduct: Visions of Gender in Victorian America*, (Oxford: Oxford University Press, 1986); Laura Lee Vance, *Seventh-Day Adventism in Crisis: Gender and Sectarian Change in an Emerging Religion* (Champaign, IL: University of Illinois Press, 1999).

2 "Online Archives," Office of Archives, Statistics, and Research of the Seventh-day Adventist Church, accessed May 10, 2018, http://documents.adventistarchives.org/default.aspx.

3 Details about the history of the digital archives are not readily available on the SDA websites. This description is based on an email exchange with the manager of the Adventist Digital Li-

This work was supported first by the Ellen G. White Estate and then by the Office of Archives, Statistics, and Research (ASTR) of the General Council of the denomination. The digitization efforts of the denomination continue to expand with the creation of the Adventist Digital Library, which seeks to "spread the gospel of Jesus Christ to the world through direct and unlimited access to Adventist historical materials," and aggregates content from a range of SDA organizations, including the General Conference, the White Estate, and many of the Adventist colleges and universities.[4]

The SDA was a prolific denomination during its first seventy years in terms of periodical production. Print served as a central mechanism by which early members, many of whom were geographically dispersed, connected with one another and created a community of believers.[5] The first publications were produced by Ellen White's husband, James, and as the denomination grew, members established new publishing houses as part of their missionary activities. Starting in the 1860s, subject-focused periodicals began to proliferate, such as the *Health Reformer*, and with a reorganization of the denomination around 1900, local and regional conferences began to produce their own titles for community news to supplement the large denominational publications. The amount of published materials, much of which has been digitized, poses something of a challenge of abundance for the textual analysis of the literature of the denomination.[6] While computational methods enable scholars to work with much larger scales of content and in different ways than are possible for human readers alone, it is helpful to focus the collection under evaluation to achieve more interpretable results.

I focused my analysis on materials published within the United States, and specifically on content produced within four main centers of denominational activity: the Great Lakes region; California and the surrounding southwest states; Washington, D.C., and the surrounding mid-Atlantic states; and the states at the southern end of the Mississippi river basin. These four areas mark the shift-

---

brary. C. Eric Koester, "RE: Inquiry Regarding Data from the Adventist Digital Library," October 26, 2017.
4 "About," Adventist Digital Library, 2018, https://adventistdigitallibrary.org/about.
5 This process parallels the development of national identity through the creation of an "imagined community" as described by Benedict Anderson. Benedict R. O'G. Anderson, *Imagined Communities: Reflections on the Origin and Spread of Nationalism*, Rev. and extended ed., 2nd ed. (London; New York: Verso, 1991).
6 Roy Rosenzweig, "Scarcity or Abundance? Preserving the Past in a Digital Era," *The American Historical Review* 108, no. 3 (June 2003), http://www.historycooperative.org/journals/ahr/108.3/rosenzweig.html.

ing centers of power and missionary activity within the denomination, as the denomination moved their headquarters from Michigan to Washington, D.C., and as the center of health reform shifted from Michigan to California as John Harvey Kellogg and the Battle Creek Sanitarium fell from favor. Additionally, apart from regional and college papers, nearly all the major periodicals of the denomination were produced from within these four geographic regions. Using these constraints, I limited my corpus for analysis to the thirty periodical titles produced in these four regions and available as digital files from the ASTR website.

The transformation of the collection of documents into data was made simpler because the periodical scans available through the ASTR had already been converted into machine readable data using OCR (Optical Character Recognition). This enabled me to extract the text, which served as my primary data set, and use machine learning algorithms to identify patterns of language use. My data consists of 13,340 periodicals issues, comprised of 197,943 pages of material, 244,564,660 total words, and 1,537,257 unique words.

This scale of content is best described as "medium" sized data—not so large that it could not be processed by a single reader with enough time, but large enough that it is difficult to interpret without some sort of overview or summary data. To find patterns within my corpus, I used topic modeling, an unsupervised classification algorithm that groups words into an arbitrary number of "topics" based on their co-occurrence within documents.[7] Unsupervised in this case means that I passed all the documents to the algorithm with no contextual information other than the number of topics to divide the words into and some additional parameters controlling the way the algorithm processed the data. The main alternative to unsupervised is supervised learning, where a researcher identifies pages as containing, say, "domestic" content, "health" content, or "theological" content, and then uses an algorithm to identify the features that distinguish those categories from one another, and then uses that model to predict the category of future materials.

Topic models generate a high-level overview of a corpus of literature, using patterns in word usage to identify different topics or subjects of discourse. Developed initially to address the problem of identifying relevant content within the exponentially-growing universe of scientific literature, the topic model is optimized for problems of information retrieval and summary. Although it works best with the more regular and topically-focused content of academic journals,

---

[7] For an introduction to potential uses of topic modeling in theological libraries, see Micah Saxton, "A Gentle Introduction to Topic Modeling Using Python," *Theological Librarianship* 11, no. 1 (April 5, 2018): 18–27.

it has been used to explore the content of a range of textual artifacts, including novels, poetry, newspapers, and diaries.[8]

MALLET was one of the early libraries released for creating topic models, and has had wide adoption within the digital humanities community because of its (relatively) easy to use interface. As researchers have begun to experiment with topic models for modeling relationships between textual features and variables such as the gender of an author, the time of publication, and other metadata aspects, new and more complex versions of the algorithm have been released. These libraries, such as Structural Topic Model (STM) and Dynamic Topic Model (DTM), factor in these different relationships as part of the model, and provide tools for computing the effect of the different variables on the topic distribution. This enables a statistical calculation of the effect of different variables on structure of the model, such as the effect of new source on the frequency and type of coverage for a topic.[9]

For my dissertation, I used the more basic topic modeling algorithm of MALLET to reduce the complexity of the algorithmic assumptions at play in tracking the discourse of the denomination over time. Modeling the relationship between discourse and time is not straightforward, and as demonstrated by Ben Schmidt, the model of change over time assumed in more complex topic modeling algorithms is one of gradual and continuous change. Such models do not account well for moments of historic rupture or for communities where a cyclical pattern

---

[8] Some high-profile projects in the digital humanities that use topic modeling on a range of different types of content include Ted Underwood and Andrew Goldstone's exploration of the archives of the *PMLA* journal, Lisa Rhody's study of ekphrasis poetry, Robert Nelson's work with the Richmond *Daily Dispatch* and Sharon Block's work with the *Pennsylvania Gazette*, and Cameron Blevins's explorations of Martha Ballard's diary. Andrew Goldstone and Underwood, Ted, "What Can Topic Models of PMLA Teach Us About the History of Literary Scholarship?," *Journal of Digital Humanities* 2, no. 1 (2012), http://journalofdigitalhumanities.org/2-1/what-can-topic-models-of-pmla-teach-us-by-ted-underwood-and-andrew-goldstone/; Lisa M. Rhody, "Topic Modeling and Figurative Language," *Journal of Digital Humanities* 2, no. 1 (April 7, 2013), http://journalofdigitalhumanities.org/2-1/topic-modeling-and-figurative-language-by-lisa-m-rhody/; Robert K. Nelson, "Introduction," Mining the Dispatch, accessed August 17, 2018, http://dsl.richmond.edu/dispatch/pages/home; Sharon Block, "Doing More with Digitization," *Common-Place* 6, no. 2 (January 2006), http://www.common-place-archives.org/vol-06/no-02/tales/; Cameron Blevins, "Topic Modeling Martha Ballard's Diary," *Cameron Blevins* (blog), April 1, 2010, http://www.cameronblevins.org/posts/topic-modeling-martha-ballards-diary/.

[9] For an example of this type of research, see Margaret E. Roberts, Brandon M. Stewart, and Edoardo M. Airoldi, "A Model of Text for Experimentation in the Social Sciences," *Journal of the American Statistical Association* 111, no. 515 (July 2, 2016): 988–1003, https://doi.org/10.1080/01621459.2016.1141684.

is operative.¹⁰ For early Seventh-day Adventists, time was not a static category of experience–time and the experience of temporality were part of what denominational members contested and were striving to understand. As a result, an algorithm with opinions about time muddies the water, so to speak, by imposing an external structure on one of the very aspects that I am looking to explore.

Having gathered an appropriate data set and selected a processing algorithm, my final processing step was to create the topic model. I selected two hundred and fifty as the target number of topics and to improve the quality of the model, limited the documents passed to MALLET to pages with more than three hundred words and error rates under ten percent. Rather than use an existing wordlist, which is the default MALLET process for removing high frequency but low meaning words, I used another topic modeling library, Gensim, to identify those words that occurred in more than sixty percent of documents (high frequency words) and those that occurred in fewer than twenty documents (low frequency words) and used that list as my stopwords list. Using this method, I generated a word list appropriate to the specialized language of the SDA. My final result was a model with some overlap in topics, but with enough specificity to serve as a useful guide to the content of the periodical pages in my study.

Generating a topic model is the first part of the challenge; using and interpreting a topic model within historical analysis is a second and less commonly discussed project. For classification problems, where a researcher uses the model to generate and assign topical categories to different documents, outputs such as the breakdown of topic percentages for each document allow the researcher to identify the most prevalent topics in each document, and use the associated label as a descriptive tag or category.¹¹ Topic models also provide an overview

---

10 Benjamin M. Schmidt, "Words Alone: Dismantling Topic Models in the Humanities," *Journal of Digital Humanities* 2, no. 1 (2012), http://journalofdigitalhumanities.org/2-1/words-alone-by-benjamin-m-schmidt/.

11 It is important to note that topic labels are an additional interpretive layer created by the user, but are not part of the topic model output. One common automated labeling strategy is to take the top five words for each topic to serve as the label. This strategy has the advantage of being fast and, with the right content, relatively easy to interpret. For more detailed uses of the topic label, however, it is desirable to move beyond the words clustered together by the model to a label that provides an interpretation of those words and the documents where those topics are prevalent. For example, the top six words of topic #45 (kingdom shall king daniel great prophecy) and topic #215 (daniel vision week end dan prophecy) from *A Gospel of Health and Salvation* are difficult to distinguish with an automatically generated label. However, when interpreted in the context of a larger sample of the topic words and the documents where these topics are prevalent, it becomes apparent that topic #45 captures documents that strongly feature the figures (the beasts, Nebuchadnezzar's statue, etc.) of the book of Daniel, while topic

of topic distributions across the entire set of documents, providing a snapshot of the major and minor themes in a corpus. As a form of machine learning, topic models can be used to classify new content, enabling researchers to use a previously generated model to classify previously unseen content.

Researchers in the digital humanities have pursued several different strategies to bridge the computational and abstract data of topic models with the interpretive questions of the humanities. My goal in working with a topic model is not to argue for correlations between different facets of SDA discourse, but to surface broad patterns and identify areas for further research. This use of a computational model fits within the epistemological commitments of the humanities, with its emphasis on complexity, multiple causality, and the idiographic, rather than using the model to argue for correlations between discourse patterns and metadata variables.[12] My primary areas of interest are within the humanities —finding ways to explore particular aspects of religious culture, to understand how a belief system works and changes, and to consider how those patterns of thought have been built upon to shape the current cultural landscape. These are questions that I believe computational models and methods can help in the exploration of, but as one method among others, including traditional archival research and narrative construction.

Approaching the topic model as an abstraction of general patterns in the periodical literature of the denomination, I focused on those topics that contained language I identified as relating to general concerns about the end times, or eschatological topics. For early Seventh-day Adventist authors, discussions of the end of time tended to rely on illusions and metaphors, particularly using biblical language from Daniel and Revelation, as well as discussions of the significance

---

#215 captures documents focused on parsing the meaning of dates in the prophetic books of Daniel and Revelation. While a longer process that requires subject-matter knowledge, this approach results in more meaningful labels that reflect both the words within the topic and the documents described.

[12] Tanya Clement provides a useful discussion of the need to explicitly link computational methods to the epistemological frameworks of the humanities as part of the process of connecting such work to the larger intellectual tradition in Tanya Clement, "Where Is Methodology in Digital Humanities?," in *Debates in the Digital Humanities*, ed. Lauren F. Klein and Matthew K. Gold, 2016 ed. (Minneapolis: University of Minnesota Press, 2016), http://dhdebates.gc.cuny.edu/debates/text/65. This is not to say that one cannot pursue a social-scientific study of traditionally humanities subject areas, such as literary history, where one uses computational methods to statistically model and argue for the relationships between different aspects of one's data. However, this is not the approach I am pursuing with the periodical literature of the SDA, choosing instead to use the computational data for description and as a guide to interpretive research.

of the dates and periods of times described in the Bible. A second set of topics that I identified were those related to eschatology, including descriptions of the second coming, heaven, and the events of the last days, as well as more theological topics such as conditional immortality and the sanctuary doctrine.[13] Third, I identified those topics that captured concerns regarding "signs of the times," the purported evidence of prophecy being fulfilled and the threats of growing disorder. Finally, I identified topics related to the separation of church and state, and particularly the Sabbath reform attempts of the late nineteenth century, which greatly concerned Seventh-day Adventist authors as both a challenge to their faith and a sign of the coming end.

Within these topical categories, I identified twenty-four topics generated by the model as linked to discussions around end-times topics. I then aggregated the prevalence of these topics over time, computing the percentage of tokens assigned to the topics in each year, both across the entire corpus and within the main denominational periodicals. (See figures 2 and 3.) This yearly aggregation of topic assignments is an additional layer of abstraction on top of the topic model, one that helps illuminate general patterns. It is important to note that aggregating topics over time can be done in multiple ways, including finding the average prevalence of a topic in each year, measuring the proportion of documents where the topic is dominant, and computing the aggregated percentage of tokens assigned to each topic in a year. Each mode of aggregation provides a different abstraction of the topic model, useful for exploring different questions of the data. The resulting patterns indicate a shift in the language of end-times expectation over time, from more explicit discussions of theology early in the denomination's history to an increased focus on precipitating events later in the period. The charts show spikes in these topics between 1851 and 1862, during the early 1870s, the years around 1890, and the period of World War I.

Seventh-day Adventist theologian Jon Paulien has documented over twenty formal predictions of the second coming throughout the history of Seventh-day Adventism, including in 1844, 1845, 1851, 1884, 1888, 1894, and 1918.[14] Overall, the model reflects periods of heightened discussion of end-times in the years prior to these formal dates, particularly in the early and later years of this study. The topic model diverges from the predictions documented by Paulien between 1860 and the mid 1880s, where the model indicates additional waves of

---

[13] For more on these theological positions, which are distinctive to the SDA, see Malcolm Bull and Keith Lockhart, *Seeking a Sanctuary*, 2nd ed. (Bloomington: Indiana University Press, 2007), http://www.jstor.org.mutex.gmu.edu/stable/j.ctt1b349jq, particularly chapters 4 and 5.

[14] Jon Paulien, *What the Bible Says About the End-Time* (Hagerstown, MD: Review & Herald Publishing Association, 1998), 20–23.

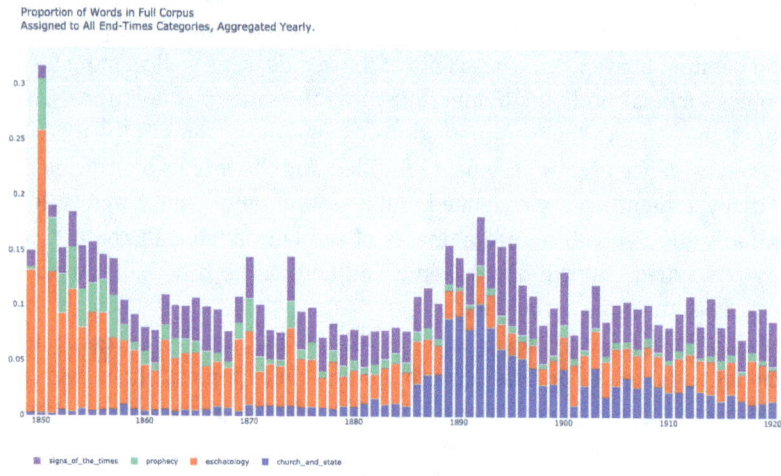

Figure 1: Combined prevalence of end-times topics in all periodical titles, except Youths' Instructor.

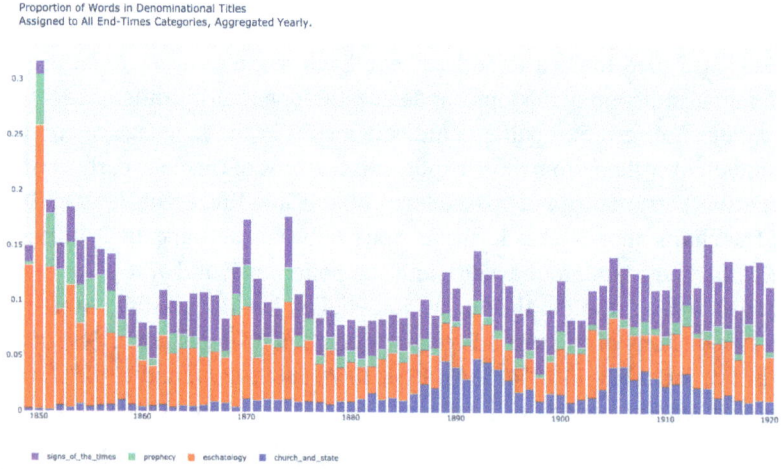

Figure 2: Combined prevalence of end-times topics in five major denominational titles Review and Herald; Signs of the Times; Adventist Review Anniversary Issues; Present Truth and The Adventist Review; and The Church Officers Gazette.

heightened expectation but shows lower than expected levels of interest in end-times during the early 1880s. This disconnect between the model and the secondary literature indicates a point for further analysis to better understand the patterns of language use that the model has captured and to examine how these two seemingly conflicting pieces of information relate to one another.

Using the topic model also allows me to dig deeper into the discourse of denominational members during these cycles of expectation and disappointment. This is where an unsupervised text mining algorithm is particularly useful. A more traditional method of finding such patterns would be to read through a range of periodicals to locate examples of "end times" discourse, and to discuss the patterns seen across the gathered examples. This is a time-intensive process and a selective one. To then examine the co-occurring shifts in discourse surrounding these discussions would require additional surveys through the literature. Topic modeling, as a guide to sources, provides an alternative method for identifying related topics within primary materials. Because I used the topic model to categorize all the text, not just those pages related to end-times discussions, and because I did not set those categories prior to categorization, I can use the model to expand my study beyond the question of when end-times expectation was particularly intense to what other topics were of concern prior to and after these periods of heightened expectation, and what that reveals about the cultural development of the SDA.

Topic modeling, as with all computational analysis in the humanities, provides new forms of evidence and new modes of investigation but does not in and of itself provide answers to the questions of meaning and interpretation that are the primary focus of scholarship in the humanities. As data to be used in the process of meaning-making, the strength of that data is dependent upon the underlying source data, the handling of that data, and the methods used in analysis. My contention is that this relationship between the creation of the model and its use in interpretive work necessitates that the technical work be treated not as background, preprocessing work, but as core to the intellectual activity that is scholarship in fields such as the digital humanities. As such, the work of data creation and processing results in scholarly products that open new areas of research, that ground the interpretive claims of the resulting narratives, and that require their own processes around publishing and preservation.

2 Current Challenges for Computational Text Analysis in Religious History

Online archives of digitized material enabled the kind of computational research I performed with the periodical literature of the SDA, but the use of this data is not without its challenges. Early digitization projects were primarily focused on increasing access and discoverability of archival materials. To support these goals, early research on the textual data from scanned materials focused on the robustness of keyword searching in the face of OCR errors and on the creation of item-level metadata sufficient for document retrieval.[15] These goals were a necessary priority in the effort to create and disseminate digital resources. However, computational analysis, such as what I undertook for my dissertation, creates new requirements on digital and digitized data sources, with needs for cleaner textual data and more expansive supporting metadata. By and large, these requirements are not being met with the first-generation work of digitization that is distributed by large scale vendors such as ProQuest and Gale, and through smaller digital archives, such as the Adventist Digital Library. To illustrate these shifting data needs, it is necessary to discuss the less glamorous work I undertook to evaluate and prepare the textual data for analysis, as well as the limitations on the types of analysis possible due to the quality of the data. My goal here is not to criticize current digital resources, but to draw attention to the ways computational analysis changes the requirements for digital resources and point to the possibilities for ongoing collaboration between researchers, archivists, and librarians in meeting these changing data needs.

My first concern with the data from the ASTR, and with any online database, was coverage, or how well the digitized materials reflected the original print materials. Since I am working with periodicals, this included both missing issues within digitized periodical titles, and which of the published titles were available in digital formats. Using the data from the file names, I charted the number of issues per year for each of the thirty titles I had identified. This provided me with an overall view of the corpus, and revealed a few trends that have shaped my analysis. First, while the primary denominational publication, *The Review and Herald*, has good coverage during nearly every year of my study, smaller periodicals, such as *The Youth's Instructor* which was written for the children of the denomination, are much less consistently available over the period. (See Figure 3.) In addition, the total number of periodicals expands drastically in the second half of my period, as regional and topical periodicals began to flourish. These material realities of the historical record shape the possibilities for analysis. In the case of computational analysis, because absences and abundances are mag-

---

15 Patrick Spedding, "'The New Machine': Discovering the Limits of ECCO," *Eighteenth-Century Studies* 44, no. 4 (2011): 437–53; Kazem Taghva, Thomas Nartker, and Julie Borsack, "Information Access in the Presence of OCR Errors," in *Proceedings of the 1st ACM Workshop on Hardcopy Document Processing*, HDP '04 (New York, NY, USA: ACM, 2004), 1–8, https://doi.org/10.1145/1031442.1031443.

nified as the sources are translated into data, it is vital to identify the strengths and weaknesses of the digital corpus, and to use that information in the processing and interpretation of the resulting computational models.

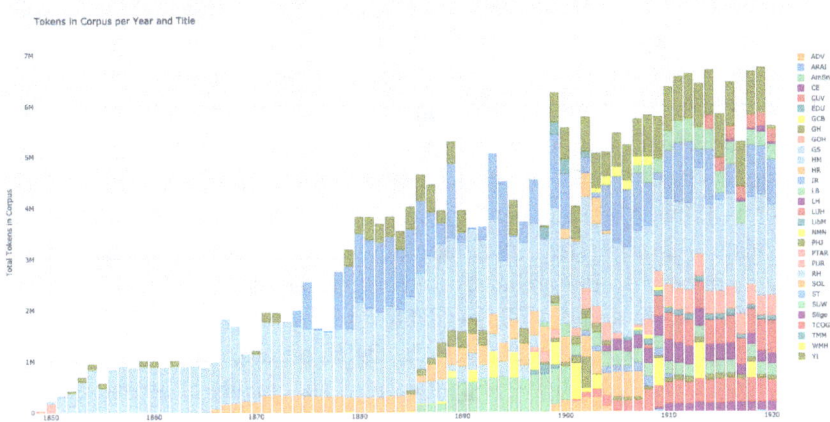

Figure 3: Chart of periodical issues digitized by the SDA and included as part of the textual analysis.

The second challenge in evaluating the coverage of my corpus was to identify the correspondence between the digitized archive and the original publication records of the denomination. For this, I used the yearbooks published by the denomination starting in 1883 to compare the record of periodicals produced by the denomination with those available in the online databases. I found that all the major titles produced by the denomination from my regions of study had a presence in the digital archive and approximately 63 percent of all major and local periodicals titles were available in digital archive.[16] This breadth of coverage is notably high, with the digital record providing a broad sample of the periodical literature circulating among denomination members. The coverage is also constrained, however, by the interests of the denomination. John Harvey Kellogg's *Good Health* publication, for example, is included within the digital archive up until 1907, when he was disfellowshiped, even though the publication itself

---

16 This percentage drops to 55% if college periodicals are included, which is unsurprising given that student publications tend to be informal and more likely to push against the main denominational positions.

continued to be published through the 1940s.[17] This reflection of theological concerns within the digital archive is not surprising, but also constitutes necessary context when interpreting the patterns captured in the model.

As reliance on digital materials expands for both traditional and computational research in the humanities, making available documentation regarding the context of those efforts is an important step to support research in this medium. Similar to the need to document provenance of archival materials, the relationship between digital sources and the archival materials is an important consideration when working with historical sources. There are always gaps in the historical record, and those gaps have generally been enlarged within digital collections. While it is incumbent upon researchers to be aware of and account for archival absences, there are opportunities for collaboration between researchers, librarians, and archivists in creating, releasing, and maintaining records of the known and digitally available resources for analysis.

The second point of concern with the digital artifacts and textual data generated for search and retrieval is data quality. The quality of textual data produced via OCR is a known concern for text-analysis projects. Two recent studies where researchers evaluated the quality of the text data generated from newspaper scans using OCR demonstrate the methods for evaluating the quality of the data. *Mapping Texts*, which set out to create an interface for the content of the Texas newspapers in the Library of Congress collection, evaluated the textual data by comparing the words in a sample of the extracted text against the Aspell spell-check program.[18] Even after some basic cleaning of the texts, the team found the word recognition rate to range from 86 % for the titles with the highest quality data to 52% for the lowest quality titles.[19] A second study, this one undertaken by a team based at King's College London, took a different approach to ascertaining OCR accuracy, calculating the best accuracy rates achieved from OCR of nineteenth century newspapers in the British Library collection. They did this by comparing samples of the OCR generated text to transcriptions of the newspaper text. On average, this study computed an overall word accuracy of 78 %, and a "significant word" accuracy—content words excluding stop words – of

---

[17] There are a few exceptions to the observation: six issues from 1937 and one from 1942 are also available at the Adventist Online Archives. But overall, the publication drops out of the SDA's online record in 1907.
[18] Andrew J. Torget et al., "Mapping Texts: Combining Text-Mining and Geo-Visualization to Unlock the Research Potential of Historical Newspapers," Whitepaper (National Endowment for the Humanities), http://mappingtexts.org/index17dc.html?page_id=271, p.15.
[19] Torget et al., "Mapping Texts," p. 23.

68.4% for the 19th Century Newspaper collection.[20] While OCR is a necessary mechanism when working with scanned objects at scale, these error rates are high enough to raise serious questions about the reliability of this data.[21]

Because many of the PDF files were created by volunteers, there is little documentation as to the OCR processes and expected quality of the textual data for the periodicals of the SDA. A quick read through the text files indicated that, while overall the text appeared readable, there were enough errors to raise questions about the OCR quality across the entire corpus. To evaluate the textual data, I pursued a similar approach to that of the *Mapping Texts* team, comparing the tokens in the OCRed text to an authoritative wordlist. This entailed creating a wordlist that was appropriate to the language of the denominational periodicals. Standard wordlists are compiled from modern English dictionaries and are appropriately conservative in their inclusion of words. However, they proved insufficient for working with the printed literature of the denomination, which is heavy in language from theology, nineteenth century medicine, and educational theory. Starting from a base wordlist from the SCOWL database, and working through the lists of frequently identified errors, I created a SDA wordlist, which I used to evaluate the tokens that appeared in the text and which served as a baseline to evaluate the success of my error correction measures.[22] After some cleaning of the texts, the percentage of verified tokens ranged from 98.6% overall rate for the cleanest periodical title to 92.2% overall rate for the title with the most errors.

Overall, these error rates are low, particularly when compared to the data reported by the "Mapping Texts" team. This low rate can be attributed in part to

---

20 The authors note that in their experience a word accuracy above 80% is best for search and retrieval tasks, a threshold that these results fall beneath. In addition, other studies have shown that more complex textual processes, such as word ranking, are more sensitive to OCR errors than search and retrieval tasks, as errors tend to increase the number of identified tokens, thereby affecting the measure prevalence of individual words. See Kazem Taghva, Thomas Nartker, and Julie Borsack, "Information Access in the Presence of OCR Errors," in *Proceedings of the 1st ACM Workshop on Hardcopy Document Processing*, HDP '04 (New York: ACM, 2004), 1–8, https://doi.org/10.1145/1031442.1031443, p. 2.

21 Ongoing work, such as the recently funded "History and Multilingual OCR" study at Northeastern University, are beginning to systematically tackle these questions surrounding OCR data for textual analysis. https://ocr.northeastern.edu/

22 SCOWL, or Spell Check Oriented Wordlists, provides numerous wordlists divided into different categories and sizes for use in creating spell check applications. The final wordlist for *A Gospel of Health and Salvation* included the base SCOWL dictionary, words from the King James Bible taken from Project Gutenberg, US city names, and a list of SDA people and places which I had compiled from the SDA yearbooks. Kevin Atkinson, *Spell Checking Oriented Word Lists (SCOWL)*, version 2016.11.20, http://app.aspell.net/create.

the use of a comprehensive dictionary against which to compare the text. In addition, it is important to note that because I am evaluating the text against known words rather than the original text, this method does not capture a range of OCR errors. Some examples of the types of errors this approach is blind to include "errors" in character recognition that create verified words, marks correctly captured spelling errors in the original as OCR errors, and errors in layout recognition, which is one of the largest problems in the OCR transcriptions. However, the statistics provide a measure of the percentage of "real word" tokens in the periodical texts and serve as a useful proxy for the quality of the OCR.

After evaluating and cleaning the text, and comparing the results to the original PDF documents, I determined that the text was a good proxy for the original scans, but also that the errors in layout recognition left the text as more of a "bag of words" representation of the periodical pages rather than a digital re-creation of the original print. This quality of the textual data shaped the types of analysis that were most effective. While processes such as search and retrieval, which rely on word recognition, have been found to be generally robust in the face of OCR errors, analysis that requires more complex weighting of words, such as computing the term frequency-inverse document frequency (TF-IDF), are more sensitive to OCR errors that skew the total number of tokens in the documents.[23] Additionally, analysis that relies on word order, such as part-of-speech tagging and named entity recognition, was unreliable due to the prevalent errors in the textual data.

This labor of evaluating and remediating the text is part of the hidden cost of computational analysis in the humanities. The scale of work that I undertook was necessary because the quality of the textual data influenced the types of analysis the data could reliably support. For the ASTR, the primary goal for the digitized text was to increase discoverability and access of the primary source materials, with the text layer providing added convenience rather than serving as the main output. Other digitized collections have focused on the textual layer as the primary product, such as the digitization of the Richmond *Daily Dispatch*.[24] The process of creating clean textual data, however, is labor-inten-

---

[23] Kazem Taghva, Thomas Nartker, and Julie Borsack, "Information Access in the Presence of OCR Errors," in *Proceedings of the 1st ACM Workshop on Hardcopy Document Processing*, HDP '04 (New York: ACM, 2004), 1–8, https://doi.org/10.1145/1031442.1031443, p. 2

[24] The vendor specifications for the digitization and rekeying of the *Dispatch* scans provides a clear example of the amount of labor involved in producing clean textual data from historical artefacts. See University of Richmond Libraries, "Background Information | Project Information," *Richmond Daily Dispatch*, accessed August 17, 2018, http://dlxs.richmond.edu/d/ddr/

sive, expensive, and offers few rewards within the current academic structure for the researchers, librarians, and archivists who undertake it.[25] At the same time, it is this carefully created textual data that is needed as computational text analysis moves from a mode of exploration to a robust mode of analysis within the humanities.

3 Towards Future Computational Research in the Study of Religion

The data made available by the SDA is an excellent example of early digitization work that can support computational analysis, and the abundance of digital content related to the history of the SDA is envy-worthy for historians looking to do computational analysis. While the Library of Congress has supported the digitization of newspapers and library vendors make some of their digitized content available for text analysis, these sources start with those materials that appeal to the broadest possible audiences.[26] For research in the history of religion, by contrast, the availability of digital sources is generally dependent upon the efforts and resources of individual denominations and the work of smaller theological libraries and archives. Having access to an abundance of digital materials, such as those published by the ASTR, makes possible computational analysis with historical data.

However, as I have shown, even with this abundance of digital data there is much work involved in constructing digital studies of religion. Additionally, there are numerous opportunities for collaboration in the creation of data, algorithms, and methods for publication, dissemination, and preservation of complex digital humanities artifacts. Early work in the digitization of archival collections has primarily focused on problems of access and information retrieval—of helping raise awareness of the contents of a collection and enabling search access within and across collections. This work has made it possible for individual

---

proinfo/bginfo.html and specifically, Andrew Rouner, "Vendor Specifications for Digitization and Rekeying" (Richmond: University of Richmond, 2005), http://dlxs.richmond.edu/d/ddr/docs/info/vendorspec.pdf.

25 The work of editing and publishing textual data is not always without its recognition and rewards, as the ongoing success of projects such as the Women Writers Project attest. "About the WWP," Women Writers Project, accessed August 18, 2018, https://www.wwp.northeastern.edu/.

26 Library of Congress, "About Chronicling America," Chronicling America, accessed August 18, 2018, https://chroniclingamerica.loc.gov/about/.

researchers such as myself to begin to undertake projects based in computational analysis.

In closing this chapter, I would like to draw on my dissertation experiences to suggest additional areas of research and scholarship that will further the possibilities for and the quality of computational research in the study of religion. First, as my work preparing the textual data from the SDA periodicals indicates, there is a need for increased attention to the creation and dissemination of textual data optimized for computational analysis. This is not to say that all digitization projects should require the detailed XML tagging undertaken in projects such as the *Richmond Daily Dispatch*. While detailed tagging may open additional options for analysis, the more basic need is for the creation of clean data that accurately captures the text of the source documents. The existence of such textual data, while labor intensive to create, greatly improves computational work and makes possible additional research in algorithm creation and analysis.[27] Such data would support the expansion and maturation of computational analysis with historic sources, and would also increase opportunities for the development of subject-specific tools to expand the options for natural language processing with the specialized language of religious literature.

A second area for further scholarly work is in the creation and dissemination of subject-specific datasets for the study of religion. Well-structured and documented data sets are themselves works of interpretation and analysis, and are scholarly products that would benefit from the collaboration of researchers, librarians, and archivists. Such datasets could include membership roles, editors and locations for publications, the location of houses of worship and other institutions, lists of authorized publications, and the like. As such data increases, the opportunities for surfacing patterns within and across religious groups also expand, but each such dataset represents large commitments of time to reliably produce. Similar to edited volumes, the creation of datasets for historical analysis should be considered an act of scholarship, and one that is done collaboratively.

The third and final area for further scholarship which I wish to note is the need to study and adapt machine learning algorithms and other computational tools for use with historical content and humanities questions. Standard natural language processing tasks, such as named entity recognition, work best when

---

[27] Clean here does not mean "normalized" or corrected. The decision of how to address errors within the original, such as typographical errors or misspellings, depends on the research questions at hand and so should be determined by the individual researcher. For commentary of the trouble of normalized text, see Katie Rawson and Trevor Muñoz, "Against Cleaning," Curating Menus, July 6, 2016, http://curatingmenus.org/articles/against-cleaning/.

trained on data that is similar to the data one is looking to process. The standard models for part-of-speech tagging and named entity recognition, however, have been trained on primarily twentieth century and news-related content. Studies evaluating their effectiveness with "out of domain" content, which constitutes most of what is used within the humanities, show a marked decline in accuracy.[28] The development of new algorithms itself is dependent upon the availability of significant amounts of clean textual data. Again, all of this work is labor intensive and interpretive, but vital for there to be a robust "digital humanities" beyond experimentation with new technologies.

The digital humanities have been accused of being just another manifestation of the commercialization and commodification of education and the humanities, and while I generally disagree with that assessment, there are dangers of embracing the "move fast and break things" attitudes of the technology sphere. The areas of work I am proposing here are labor intensive, complex, and require care and imagination, and they are less attractive as they require revisiting ground that is known. Rather than finding the "next new thing" that will illuminate patterns, I am proposing slowing down, clarifying methodology so that the scholarly contributions are understandable, and doing the necessary work of modifying and "refactoring" existing methods to work well with the unique content of religious studies.

The change in emphasis from quick adoption to long term cultivation is also why I see these areas as places where collaborations between researchers, librarians, and archivists can thrive. Datasets are formed to answer questions. There must be research needs behind the creation of text, data, and computational models. At the same time, librarians and archivists have the expertise in data management and preservation, the infrastructure to support and preserve these artifacts as scholarly outputs, and the field awareness needed to make such work viable and useful beyond individual projects. Where the digital humanities are at their most productive is in encouraging collaboration and offering alternatives to existing academic hierarchies. My work for my dissertation highlights that there is much research yet to do to enable robust applications of computational methods to the study of religion.

---

28 David Bamman, "Natural Language Processing for the Long Tail," 2017, http://people.ischool.berkeley.edu/~dbamman/pubs/pdf/dh2017.pdf.

II **The Database as Locus of Digital Humanities**

Tracy Miller
Digital Humanities and the Interdisciplinary Database: Confronting the Complexity of Chinese Religious Architecture in the Academic Marketplace

As most of us now realize, the use of digital tools to engage in computational, interdisciplinary research in the humanities holds the potential to transform our understanding of the human condition, past and present. However, in order to take advantage of the power of digital tools, data previously constructed for publication in book form must be reconceptualized for both analog and digital consumption. The success of a young digital humanities scholar, one who is required to produce peer-reviewed publications for tenure and promotion, is partially dependent on clarifying the front-end time commitment of tool development and data entry necessary for the development of current digital projects. The dynamic, trial-and-error nature of the field can make even this task difficult. However, as more and more tools are developed for the study of the material culture of religion, selecting the appropriate items and reorganizing them for customized applications promises new ways of researching and understanding the historical past. The collaborative culture of digital humanities increasingly allows for the development of more efficient ways to produce tangible results so that younger scholars can succeed in both project and career.

This essay is a documentation of my experience developing *Architectura Sinica*, a digital humanities project designed to facilitate research in medieval Chinese temple culture. I will begin by providing a background to the project scope and associated image archives to give a sense of the nature of art historical teaching and research tools, past and present. I will then discuss my efforts to actualize the project through the semantic web and through XQuery languages and technologies. Finally, I discuss my current application and some of the challenges I have confronted with text and image management. I hope this essay will help introduce scholars interested in beginning a digital material culture project in the academic environment to a few of the pathways forward, as well as some of the roadblocks, in computational humanities.

1 Assessing the Scope of the Project

Architectura Sinica started as a biproduct of fundamental art historical research on regional style in traditional Chinese timber-frame architecture from the Middle Period (roughly the tenth through the twelfth centuries). In my dataset, the individual buildings and sites that contained them are all dedicated to divinity worship. Most of the sites are Buddhist, but temple buildings and complexes dedicated to divinities associated with monastic Daoism, as well as Confucianism, state religion, and local cults, are included. Early on it was clear that the results of this research could be of interest to an interdisciplinary audience including art/architectural historians interested in Chinese art and global building technology, as well as historians of religion interested in material culture of ritual praxis in Asia.

My original concept seemed very simple. I wanted to create a research tool that would allow me to identify specific stylistic and structural details of these historic buildings, search by those architectural features, and map the output to determine whether stylistic differences were related more to regional distinctions or trends in an empire-wide style that changed gradually over time. In order to problematize the question of dynastic style, I chose to focus on a group of historic buildings from a particular time period rather than a dynasty. I selected the period from 900–1200 because within this date range we have sufficient extant historical remains in different areas of China to investigate variations in structure and style over space as well as time. Therefore, it seemed that the use of GPS technologies to both document the location of individual sites, buildings, and other artifacts (including sculpture and stele inscriptions) and dynamically map development over time would be a fruitful research endeavor.

To build the database it was necessary first to determine the individual component parts of the sites within the study. Traditional Chinese architecture is routinely organized into large building complexes (which I refer to as "sites"), and historic buildings within the complex are usually identified by both the name of the site as well as the name of the building itself. For example, we might have a Great Buddha Hall (individual historic building) within Dayun Cloister (larger site), which would usually be called the Dayun Cloister Great Buddha Hall. The architectural features which are the focus of my research are associated with individual buildings. Other artifacts, including sculpture, paintings, and stele with inscriptions are also contained within a site. The larger site is typically older, sometimes substantially so, than the extant buildings and other artifacts contained within it. Thus, I would need to have a separate entry or web page containing information on the site that was distinct from the web page containing information on the building. Because the terminology for the sites, buildings, and individual architectural features is unfamiliar to non-specialist readers in Chinese as well as in English or other languages we needed to have a dictionary function of some kind as a separate portion of the website.

Trained in the days of text tables and analog photography, the biggest surprise in embarking on this project was realizing I needed to fully rethink my documentation methods for the sake of computer consumption and output. By 2007 I had already completed a significant portion of the research on individual buildings, with field notes and photographs for the forty-one most important of the one hundred twenty-three complexes believed to hold authentic buildings from the period. I received an NEH grant in 2008 to develop my regional style project with the potential for building an open-access web-based research tool as part of the larger proposal. Improvements in commercial mapping systems, such as Google Earth, revealed the immediate potential of the graphic display of my GIS data, and encouraged me to consider developing the digital archive of photographs and a mapping website as a first step in my regional style project. Yet, although the tables and spreadsheets I created for my own use in books and articles were appropriate for print publication and remained good research tools, they were not appropriate for computerized data manipulation. I needed to reformat my textual data completely.

Furthermore, by 2007 technologies for producing raw images of buildings, a data source as important as textual documentation for an architectural historian, had undergone their own digital revolution and technologies for storing and manipulating those images were, and continue to be, rapidly changing. Images of the buildings I studied from 1997–2002 had all been produced as analog slides and photographs. As digital cameras improved and became more affordable in the early 2000s, the shift to born-digital images created new challenges for data storage and documentation.

Transformations in the production of images for research purposes were paralleled by the rapid shift from analog to digital in art and art history instruction, a development that directly impacted the infrastructure for research and study of cultural heritage objects. This was not the first time technological developments dramatically transformed the means by which we come to learn about the physical world around us. Photography itself, of course, began that process, and with it a field developed around the preservation and cataloging of photographic representations of cultural heritage. Within ten years of the development of photograph, plate glass was used for positive photographic transparencies, as well as negatives which would then be projected onto photographic paper. The positive transparencies could be projected onto a wall at a magnified scale with the "magic lantern," a technology for displaying images used as early as 1665. These lantern slides were quickly used for research on subjects as diverse as historic architecture and medical research.[1] Lantern slides were used for instruction in the art history classroom beginning in the late nineteenth century, and continuing at least through the 1960s, by which time 2x2" glass slides and then 35 mm slides replaced the larger-format lantern slides, and the lantern slides were relegated to the archive.[2]

The digital revolution of the early twenty-first century had a similar impact on the study and teaching of material culture. As advancements were made in scanning, digital photography, projection, and file storage, teaching with digital reproductions, which could be saved to a personal computer rather than filed in a slide library, was an obvious choice. The convenience of digital imaging was made a necessity by 2004, when Kodak discontinued the production of slide projectors.[3] Slide libraries were quickly transformed into visual resources centers for the support of slide scanning, digital image archiving, and training in the digital image presentation software now indispensable for day-to-day classroom instruction. Vanderbilt was on the cutting edge in the use of this technology, and faculty were already using digital images in virtual slide trays for classroom instruction in the 2001–2002 academic year.[4] With a move to a new facility in 2009, all art history course presentations were moved to digital platforms (mostly PowerPoint and Keynote) and the slide collection at Vanderbilt University was, like the earlier lantern slides, placed into off-campus storage. Thus, during this same period my own system for presentation and publication of images,

---

[1] Simon H. Gage, "The Introduction of Photographic Transparencies as Lantern Slides," *Journal of the Royal Society of Arts* 59.3036 (1911), 255–257.

[2] Annemarie van Roessel, "Through a Glass, Brightly: Re-viewing a Lost Architectural and Pedagogical Landscape Through Historic Lantern Slides," *Art Documentation: Journal of the Art Libraries Society of North America*, 22.1 (2003): 6. Developments in color photography in mid-century helped to reduce costs and facilitated the shift in format, see Carla Conrad Freeman, "Visualizing Art: An Overview of the Visual Resources Profession in the United States," *Art Documentation: Journal of the Art Libraries Society of North America*, 7.1 (1988): 6.

[3] Ching-Jung Chen, "Analog to Digital: Conversion of the Image Libraries at the City College of New York," *Art Documentation: Journal of the Art Libraries Society of North America*, 28.1 (2009), 36. https://web.archive.org/web/20050206010328/http://slideprojector.kodak.com/ (accessed October 25, 2018).

[4] Marshall Breeding, "A Web-Based Image Access System for Classroom Presentation in Art History," Coalition for Networked Information Project Briefings, April 17, 2002. https://www.cni.org/topics/digital-curation/a-web-based-image-access-system-for-classroom-presentation-in-art-history (accessed January 18, 2019).

the primary source data on which my argument hinged, needed a full overhaul as well.

I realized that I needed to restructure my data for two purposes: efficiency of cataloging numerous images of buildings and artifacts tied to a temple site, for which a relational database seemed appropriate, and managing research notes and sources on a site—all textual data—in a format that would allow for the greater understanding of regional architectural style and sharing of that information digitally. These two purposes had multiple options that I was cautioned to consider before setting up the system's architecture overall. In the end I decided that the cataloging of textual information might be better served by one set of tools and building an archive of images of objects by another. Although differently organized, information on images and artifacts could be pulled together for display through a web portal. The promise of Linked Data and SPARQL (SPARQL Protocol and RDF Query Language) that was so compelling at the beginning of the project was retained as an area of future development as all of our data can be exported in RDF (Resource Description Framework)/XML as well as TEI (Text Encoding Initiative)/XML and GeoJSON. But a lot of experimenting was necessary before I came to those conclusions.

2 Reconceptualizing Art Historical Data

The reorganization of textual data began with a fresh look at tables and spreadsheets. My fieldwork starts with photo-documenting extant premodern temple complexes and taking field notes regarding geolocation, rough building dimensions, and description of critical architectural features. Beginning in 1997 I used simple tables within the word processing program Nisus, because of its ability to handle Chinese characters. I printed these to fill in on site, and then manually input the data into my computer after returning to an indoor environment. As the MS Word suite improved its ability to handle non-Latin scripts, I began using Excel spreadsheets and, beginning in 2007–2008, I printed these in booklet form for each fieldtrip. These were necessarily compact for their use in the field, so all of the different elements I wanted to ensure were included in my fieldwork were configured to be able to print onto a single 8.5 x 11" page (Fig 1).

After deciding I wanted to engage in a computational project, I learned my spreadsheets were not machine readable. That is, while these spreadsheets were "digitized," they were not easily consumed by database programs and thus what

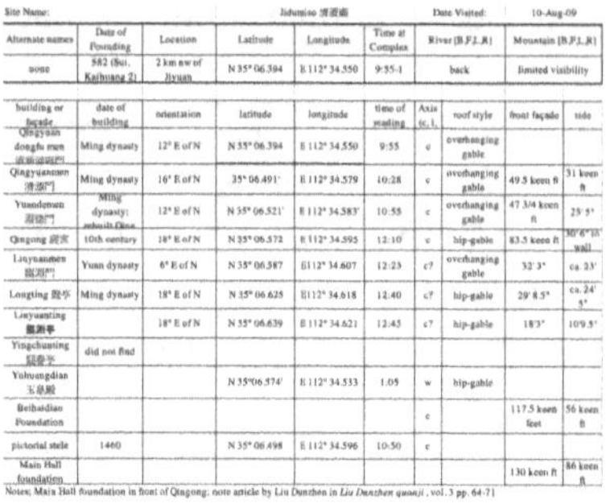

Site Name: Jidumiao 济渎庙 Date Visited: 10-Aug-09

Alternate names	Date of Founding	Location	Latitude	Longitude	Time at Complex	River [B,F,L,R]	Mountain [B,F,L,R]
none	582 (Sui, Kaihuang 2)	2 km nw of Jiyuan	N 35° 06.394	E 112° 34.550	9:55-1	back	limited visibility

building or façade	date of building	orientation	latitude	longitude	time of reading	Axis (c, l,	roof style	front façade	side
Qingyuan dongfu men 清源洞府门	Ming dynasty	12° E of N	N 35° 06.394	E 112° 34.550	9:55	c	overhanging gable		
Qingyuanmen 清源门	Ming dynasty	16° E of N	35° 06.491'	E 112° 34.579	10:28	c	overhanging gable	49.5 keen ft	31 keen ft
Yuandemen 渊德门	Ming dynasty; rebuilt Qing	12° E of N	N 35° 06.521'	E 112° 34.583'	10:55	c	overhanging gable	47 3/4 keen ft	25' 5"
Qingong 寝宫	10th century	18° E of N	N 35° 06.572	E 112° 34.595	12:10	c	hip-gable	83.5 keen ft	30' 6" in wall
Linyuanmen 临渊门	Yuan dynasty	6° E of N	N 35° 06.587	E112° 34.607	12:23	c?	overhanging gable	32' 3"	ca. 23'
Longting 龙亭	Ming dynasty	18° E of N	N 35° 06.625	E112° 34.618	12:40	c?	hip-gable	29' 8.5"	ca. 24' 5"
Linyuanting 临渊亭		18° E of N	N 35° 06.639	E 112° 34.621	12:45	c?	hip-gable	18'3"	10'9.5"
Yingchunting 迎春亭	did not find								
Yuhuangdian 玉皇殿			N 35°06.574'	E 112° 34.533	1:05	w	hip-gable		
Beihaidian Foundation						c		117.5 keen feet	56 keen ft
pictorial stele	1460		N 35° 06.498	E 112° 34.596	10:50	c			
Main Hall foundation								130 keen ft	86 keen ft

Notes: Main Hall foundation in front of Qingong; note article by Liu Dunzhen in *Liu Dunzhen quanji*, vol. 3 pp. 64-71

Figure 1: Example of site spreadsheet designed for use in the field.

I was doing was not actually "digital humanities," strictly defined.[5] After consulting first with the Vanderbilt campus GIS specialist (Jacob Thornton) and later with scholarly communications specialists (Cliff Anderson and Steve Baskauf), I learned that software developed for humanities computing, including GIS and XQuery, is often designed to consume CSV (comma-separated values) documents. Yet, while tables pose no problem for organizing my humanistic data, organizing by comma-separated values was extremely difficult for me to edit or otherwise control.

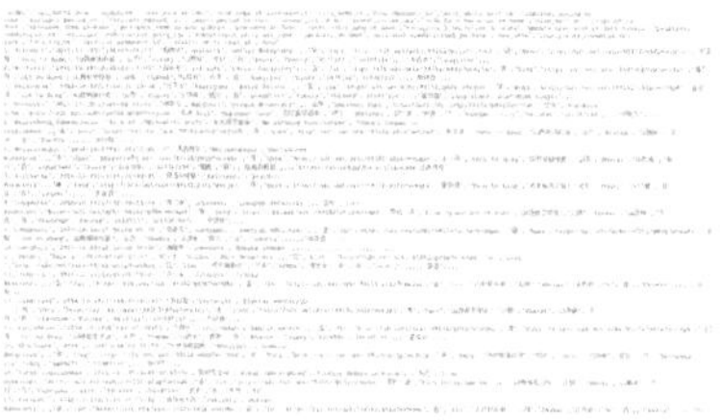

Figure 2: Screenshot of sites spreadsheet viewed in "raw" format on GitHub.

Although spreadsheets in CSV format are considered to be more user-friendly than a document in simple comma-separated values viewed without visible cells or "raw," (Fig. 2), they are still extremely cumbersome to fill and edit in analog format and consequently less functional in the field (Fig. 3).

My first experiment was to generate a map of the individual building sites in my dataset. In order to manipulate my more complex metadata, I would need to reorganize it into a simple, unformatted, two-dimensional spreadsheet. For the

5 For more on what the Digital Humanities is and is not, see Burdick, Anne, et al. "Questions and Answers: Digital Humanities Fundamentals." In *Digital Humanities*, edited by Anne Burdick, Johanna Drucker, Peter Lunenfeld, Todd Presner, and Jeffrey Schnapp (Cambridge, Mass., and London: The MIT Press, 2012), 122.

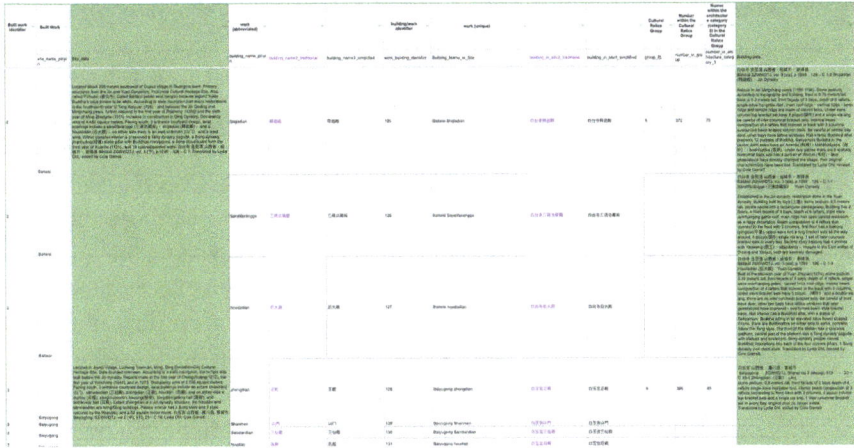

Figure 3: Screenshot of Google Sheets version of combined site/buildings spreadsheet.

map I created a flat spreadsheet with rows with a column for the name of each site, its latitude, and its longitude. I also converted the latitude and longitude taken from my hand-held GPS from analog to digital coordinates in order to be able to take advantage of mapping software like ArcGIS. Of course, once in CSV format with digital coordinates, the same spreadsheet could be used to create as many maps as I wanted, and I could write a program (or use a pre-existing one) to select any number of sites based on particular search criteria. I was reassured by one colleague that CSV is still the most stable document type, so this was not the worst way to ultimately store data and therefore not a waste of precious research time—which, to be honest, was how it felt. Still, this appeared to be a relatively straightforward task. The subsequent deconstruction and reconstruction of the rest of my data followed two paths, both of which are preserved in the *Architectura Sinica* website today.

3 Coding Nomothetic vs. Idiographic Data

The types of data organization I needed to produce my ideal web output brought into focus methodological differences between digital humanists and scientists, much like Neo-Kantian dichotomies between nomothetic and idiographic approaches to knowledge. With generalizable nomothetic data, the binary computational model is easily adaptable. Geolocation of the individual buildings, for example, went very quickly from spreadsheet to output in maps, and was also readily adaptable to RDF formatting for sharing through LOD (Linked Open

Data). For more idiographic data, especially where we wanted to build in the potential to account for multiple interpretations, XML languages provide greater potential to account for idiosyncrasies, a process more in keeping with the long tradition of textual interpretation.[6] When I began my project, participants in the working groups addressing DH topics at Vanderbilt were willing to experiment with my data in two different systems. The first was based in the promise of sharing through LOD using RDF triples, the second was the rewriting of the code according to TEI guidelines in order to be able to better document the historical and, potentially, epigraphical elements associated with my building sites.

Our Semantic Web working group was the first to take on my dataset. Led by one of the group members, biologist Steve Baskauf, my data were used to test a piece of code, the "Guid-O-Matic," that he had developed from the need to generate global unique identifiers for his Bioimages database. Interested in bioinformatics, Baskauf wrote a light program to transform flat CSV spreadsheets of his data into RDF triples for consumption through a SPARQL endpoint.[7] Having established HTTP URIs as unique identifiers for trees and other species in Bioimages, Baskauf was interested in updating the program, and I was interested to see if it might be applicable to the study of cultural heritage sites. Working with two other colleagues in the group, one from our central library (Yuh-Fen Benda) and the other from our visual resources center (William Sealy), we pulled together the essential searchable categories of objects into a spreadsheet, and developed a data model for the categories. Originally, we were hoping to be able to display the site in different languages and scripts, and so all of the text data (site names, building names, and architectural features) were described in English, traditional Chinese, and simplified Chinese.

My first spreadsheet, one which I could follow as a human, was still not really simple enough for computer consumption, and especially not for the parameters of Linked Data (Fig. 3). It was an all-encompassing single document that reflected complex relationships between an individual historic building, a larger historic building complex (or cultural heritage site), and a location with numeric (latitude/longitude) and text (modern country, province, town) reference points. For XQuery queries, searchable categories need to be considered individually. In one work-group session we discussed the relationships between the various com-

---

6 Charlotte Roueché, "Why Do We Mark Up Texts?" In *Collaborative Research in the Digital Humanities*, edited by Willard McCarty and Marilyn Deegan, 118–123 (Farnham, Surrey, England: Ashgate, 2011).
7 For more on Steve Baskauf's development of the initial Traditional Chinese Architecture Digital Research Tool, see the detailed discussion on his blog: http://baskauf.blogspot.com/2016/10/guid-o-matic-goes-to-china.html (accessed Jan. 2019).

ponents of my data to establish how we would want them to be able to relate to each other in a search. Once those relationships were mapped out (Fig. 4), Baskauf used his modified Guid-O-Matic code, GOM2, to create a web application for display. Because of the difference in the dating of sites and buildings, we needed separate spreadsheets for, and eventually also gave separate URIs to, each of the sites and each of the historic buildings (or artifacts) I had documented within the sites.

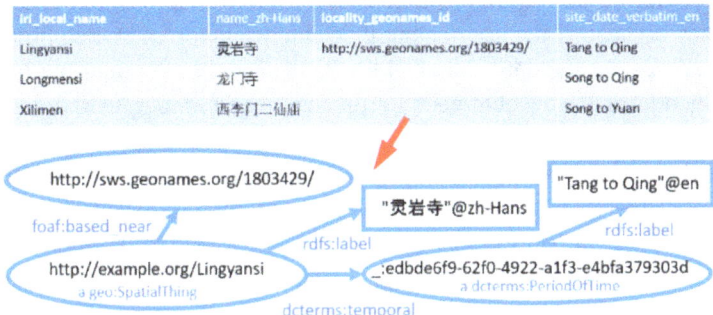

Figure 4: Bubble graph diagram and spreadsheet showing organization according to the Resource Description Framework (RDF) Source: http://baskauf.blogspot.com/2016/10/guid-o-matic-goes-to-china.html.

The promise of the Semantic Web is interoperability, and Baskauf's goal for our group was to test the possibilities of XQuery and generate RDF-formatted LOD for consumption through SPARQL queries. To that end, he posted the code on GitHub for open download and sought out external sources of LOD to import into the application whenever possible. GitHub may be openly available, but it is not user friendly for the neophyte. And although I created a GitHub account and currently happily use GitHub to edit code, its core function, cloning code for individual experimentation, remains beyond my comfort-zone. Thus, while I was involved in some of the editing, at the time I depended on the developer in our visual resources center to manage our installation of Baskauf's code.

One of the primary goals of the Semantic Web working group was to experiment with different sources of Linked Open Data. These included GeoNames (seen in Fig. 4), the Getty Thesaurus of Geographic Names (TGN), and, potentially definitions of architectural terms that could be imported from the Getty Art and Architectural Thesaurus (AAT). Baskauf was also able to import research images by linking to my Flickr Pro account, where I store my born-digital images, and mapping data through Google Earth. As an experiment, this was very exciting. He was able to quickly generate a search engine that would display satellite and map images of sites, associate them with nearby locations using GeoNames, and import PRC-generated county and province names from the TGN for location display.

I was a bit uncomfortable employing these external sources for a stable research website, however, and I still strongly question the dependability of web sources for geographic information in China. For example, although Baskauf chose 1803429 as the location for a village/town of Lingyansi, that is only one of six entries with that name in GeoNames. Even the TGN poses a challenge for consistency because of the use of simplified characters for all of the Chinese place names. While the standard character set for the People's Republic of China is the simplified format, we would need to run a conversion program in order to display those names in a fully traditional Chinese character version of the site. Furthermore, because my subject area is still in an early stage of development, there are no reliable external authorities for much of my data. The Getty AAT, for example, did not contain terminology specific to historic Chinese buildings beyond one or two words. Indeed, I began to think that my dataset was not fully reducible to a few generalizable principles, and might not ever be. In order to account for the vagaries of information about the historic past, I turned to a different database model, one that was being developed by Dave Michelson on Syriac culture. For that I needed to have a full rewrite of the site, which I renamed *Architectura Sinica*.

Truth be told, the transition from the Traditional Chinese Architecture Digital Research Tool to *Architectura Sinica* resulted as much from the desire to collaborate with Vanderbilt colleagues to develop a portable cultural heritage application as it did from frustration with the current limitations of RDF and SPARQL queries. Still, I needed to be able to document my sources for seemingly objective pieces of information, such as the beginning and end dates I chose for Chinese dynasties in my general date information. I also needed to clearly document multiple sources of interpretation and disagreement within the blocks of text describing the sites, buildings, and other artifacts. Michelson and the team that developed the "Srophe app" for the Syriac Reference Portal had resolved many of these issues when developing their website. As stated on their site, the goals of their project were to compile sources on the study of Syriac culture and facilitate wide distribution of information and tools to further the study of the subject.[8] It was written in the XML application eXist, using TEI guidelines. Like Baskauf's projects, information sharing is fundamental to their approach. The code can

---

8 http://syriaca.org/about-srophe.html (accessed January, 2019).

be forked from GitHub for individual development and publications of *Syriaca.org* are openly available under Creative Commons licensing. Although their focus was on textual data rather than physical artifacts, they were also concerned with the physicality of their material and mapping is a big part of their project.

Michelson had already worked with a colleague in our Anthropology department, Steve Wernke, to adapt the code to his research in the Andes, and it seemed fruitful to try to customize their codebase for my dataset.[9] I hired an independent developer, Winona Salesky, who had worked with Michelson and Wernke on their sites, to adapt the code for *Architectura Sinica*. Still a work in progress, during the 2018–2019 academic year, we hired a post-doctoral scholar to help regularize the code for *Architectura Sinica* and the Srophe app overall so that it conforms more closely to TEI guidelines. We are also fully documenting individual aspects so that the app might be customizable beyond the Vanderbilt campus. During the transition process I chose to make a number of simplifications based on my experience building the initial spreadsheets for TCADRT. The most significant of these was in the choice of display languages. Producing parallel sites in English, traditional Chinese, and simplified Chinese proved to be too cumbersome to edit effectively without a large team of bilingual specialists. I decided it would be better if the whole site were bilingual in English and Chinese. I also chose to use traditional characters rather than simplified. This would allow for inclusion of epigraphic information in the future, which is all written in traditional characters, and simplify editing. Yet, because we aspire to have a bilingual site, rather than a site displayed in different script sets (Roman, traditional Chinese, and simplified Chinese), I still feel comfortable using simplified characters for TGN imported geographic names. In this case it can be seen as less of a political position and more of a pragmatic one, as this is how maps generated in the target country would represent themselves.

The second change was to expand the architectural features section of the original site. My original dataset included only those architecture features I had deemed most critical to documenting stylistic change across different regions during the 900–1200 timeframe of my initial project. At first I imagined that we would be able to import other technical terms less critical to my study, such as the different building and site types common to Chinese religious architecture, to definitions in the Getty AAT using LOD through a SPARQL query.

---

9 Steve Wernke's site, developed with Jeremy Mumford, is the Linked Open Gazetteer of the Andean Region (LOGAR), see: http://www.logarandes.org/geo/about.html (accessed January, 2019).

Yet, because the Getty AAT did not have material yet on Traditional Chinese Architecture, a number of my colleagues working in Chinese architecture and I thought it might be useful to research and define important terms for submission to the AAT. The first meeting of the ATTCAT (Annotation and Translation of Traditional Chinese Architectural Terminology) Project took place on June 21–26, 2018. We are slated to publish the results of our research on *Architectura Sinica* as well as through the Getty AAT, thus the results of this project, too, are designed for consumption through Linked Open Data. For the sake of community, and interoperability, I feel good about adopting TEI guidelines as we prepare individual entries for publication on *Architectura Sinica*. The Pictorial Dictionary of Chinese Architectural Terminology will adhere to the highest academic standards in the humanities, including detailed bibliographic references and a Works Cited page so that scholars using the site will always be able to trace the source of our information. Additionally, we are working to include drawings and photographic examples of idiosyncratic elements. Determining the best method of storing high quality image files is our next big challenge.

4 For the Future: Images of Artifacts

Although a core mission of the Traditional Chinese Architecture Digital Research Tool and the later *Architectura Sinica* was to make available images of extant tenth through twelfth century buildings in China, I have yet to determine the best means to archive and curate those images for internet consumption. As I mentioned above, Baskauf's initial code pulled images from Flickr to populate the relevant pages of my site, a system we are still using. But this commercial service was not my preferred image repository, precisely because it is subject to the vagaries of the marketplace. Below I briefly outline my experience building (or, more precisely *not* building) an interoperable image archive housed at the university. I also describe potential technologies we might adopt in the future.

Having been involved in the transition from analog to digital in our own Visual Resources Center, I had originally planned to archive and catalog images using DIMLI (Digital Media Management Library), a relational database our VRC staff developed in the wake of the 2008 financial crisis. Caught in the whirlwind of the transformation from analog to digital in the early 2000s, the Visual Resources Center at Vanderbilt experimented with a number of different archiving and image-delivery systems. As mentioned above, our first in-house system used during the 2001–2002 academic year replicated the slide tray exactly. The digital slide tray files were projected individually in sequence and required two digital projectors in order to project two images for comparison. Yet, the division of labor in the traditional slide library reflected a division between well-developed methods of cataloging and archiving physical slides and the technology used to produce them. Digital images seemingly brought them together: catalogers and digital photographers were both using computers. Yet the specialized training and intellectual inclination of digital photographers and slide curators were usually different, and unlike with slides, the image delivery system was more closely tied to the tools for cataloging than the tools for projection. Quality control fell first to those responsible for cataloging images, with image quality as a secondary concern because of the costs of high-resolution image storage and projection. Early iterations of endeavors to share digitized images, particularly through the Mellon-funded Artstor, fell short in both image quality and their digital image viewer, making the shift to digital more challenging for scholars who needed high quality reproductions for their research and teaching.[10] Thus, in order to maintain a high level of instruction using the digital projector, we still needed (and still do need) to have means to produce and archive images unique to our teaching at the institutional level. We turned to MDID (Madison Digital Image Database), an open-source image repository and delivery tool for art history teaching developed at James Madison University. Although the image viewers in both Artstor and MDID were cumbersome to use, by this time the power of images in business presentations had fueled the commercial development of presentation software such as PowerPoint and Keynote and faculty quickly adopted them for everyday teaching as well as public lectures and conference presentations. Yet, funding cuts due to the 2008 financial crisis undermined development of MDID and we had to look elsewhere for our cataloging tools.

Concerns that MDID would fold due to lack of funding, coupled with a general disappointment in the quality of Artstor's Shared Shelf cataloging tool and archived images overall, inspired our VRC staff to develop their own cataloging and image retrieval tool. Artstor and MDID used flat cataloging systems, which were cumbersome to use for image cataloging. Development of our own in-house cataloging tool, DIMLI, emerged from a desire to use a relational database for our image archive to enhance speed in cataloging. It also allowed for delivery of PowerPoint-sized images to faculty for classroom and conference presentation. However, institutional backing for this project was shaky, and retaining key staff as they enhanced their own technological profiles proved to be impossible. In the interim, Artstor expanded their tool for customized university ar-

---

10 A brief history of Artstor, and its new shared digital media platform, JSTOR Forum, can be found at http://www.artstor.org/mission.

chives, originally Artstor Shared Shelf, to create JSTOR Forum, to which our teaching archive at Vanderbilt is currently being transferred. This tool can now support a relational database structure and remains a possibility for archiving my personal collection. Yet, even as I write, new image-sharing protocols are being developed for more sophisticated access to high-resolution images, including image annotation. A consortium of image repositories and research libraries is working to produce the International Image Interoperability Framework (IIIF). This system allows for remote image file viewing whereby the user can magnify a portion of an image for their research without downloading a large file to their desktop (or other) repository, among other functions.[11] Major image repositories, including Artstor, are also working to be IIIF compliant, which bodes well for increased image sharing and manipulation in the future. In the interim, Flickr is a relatively inexpensive option for simple cataloging and image retrieval. As long as the company (or its current parent, SmugMug) remains viable, my database can continue to incorporate images.

5 Conclusion: Lessons Acknowledged, If Not Yet Learned

Developing *Architectura Sinica* has provided me an opportunity to reconceive the nature of the visual data I employ in my research. This digital turn allows for a more integrated research project with the potential for a much wider reach as text and material sources on sacred sites can be analyzed together using similar tools of organization. I feel confident it will suit my immediate research needs, and I hope that its availability on the web will expand interest in and an understanding of traditional Chinese architecture. As we expand the Srophe app for a larger audience, we have to acknowledge that GitHub and XQuery require a large time commitment, perhaps too large for most non-technical people to use efficiently. One way in which we are currently addressing this concern is by developing a fillable web form for individual entries that would allow data input with no knowledge of XML languages. Ideally it will be designed so that an undergraduate working in a lab can complete entry drafts with minimal supervision and editing. I have many colleagues who would take on more digital projects if similar tools were developed in order to maximize their humanities training

---

11 For more details on the benefits of IIIF, see https://iiif.io/community/faq/#what-is-iiif (retrieved January, 2019).

and minimize the need for coding skills. One is forced to ask, is facility with XML, or RDF, a necessary qualification for the digital humanist?

As material culture becomes accessible to scholars of religion and other areas of the humanities, there will be even greater demand for a means by which to treat text as artifact and artifact as text. Increased accessibility of image and map data provides an opportunity for us to become more familiar with the complexity of the pre-modern past. IIIF encoding will greatly enhance the usability of high-quality digital reproductions, and has the potential to transform their use in the research through image annotation.

The application of digital tools for the study of religious sites will come into its own when university DH labs across the country are developed enough to include technical staff expert in industry standards for rapid digital archiving and data retrieval. This is already in place in many institutions, and will be greatly facilitated by the development of customizable open-source tools. Modification of commercial and social networking applications may be able to fast-track results, but within the university, an institution unique in its ability to generate and preserve scholarship of the highest level for the benefit of future generations, we should work to develop robust systems for high-level research independent of the fluctuations and fads of the marketplace.

Christine Schwartz
Using XQuery and XSLT to Build an Aggregation of Metadata Records for Religious Texts and Non-Print Items

1 Context and Overview of the Theological Commons Project

In early 2008, Princeton Theological Seminary started its partnership with the Internet Archive to digitize public domain print materials from our library collections. The project was initially funded by Microsoft, but within a few months Microsoft ended its mass digitization initiative.[1] The Internet Archive had already set up a scanning center in the library's building and remained after Microsoft pulled out. Over time this scanning center became one of the regional digitization centers for the Internet Archive's East Coast operations. Fortunately, the work of digitizing the library's collections has continued in earnest up to the present day.

In December 2010, the library's digital team met with the seminary's president, Dr. Iain Torrance, concerning the Internet Archive's user interface for our digitized items. He wanted the digital team to build an alternative user interface. President Torrance envisioned the creation of a simple, lightweight discovery layer for our collections that would provide focused search of theological resources and user-friendly navigation. At that meeting, President Torrance specified in broad strokes what he would like to see done with this project. The quantity of content is so great at the Internet Archive that it is hard to navigate and narrow in on the seminary's digital content. Even within our own collection page there are challenges; for example, the Internet Archive's user interface lists all the Library of Congress Subject Headings for our digitized materials. The user has to navigate through numerous pages of subject headings to find what they are looking for when conducting a subject search.

The charge for the digital team was to create this new user interface as a gateway to the Internet Archive for theological resources. We were to include broad subject categories as facets, date facets that reflected historical time peri-

---

1 Gregory P. Murray, "Featured Web Resource: Theological Commons," *Theological Librarianship* 9:2 (October 2016): 1–4, https://doi.org/10.31046/tl.v9i2.434.

ə OpenAccess. © 2021 Christine Schwartz, published by De Gruyter. This work is licensed under the Creative Commons Attribution-NonCommercial-NoDerivatives 4.0 International License.
https://doi.org/10.1515/9783110536539-007

ods, and an index of names. The subject facets were to be few in number and based on the terminology of a classical seminary education, the opposite of the presentation of the long, complex lists of subject headings. We were also going to provide a "Download to Kindle" feature, to facilitate offline reading on this popular e-book reader. Additionally, we wanted to create this new user interface as a theology portal that would include books on religion and theology from other institutions besides our own. Finally, we wanted to include a book reader in a frame, which we added in 2016. President Torrance liked the user interface we had developed for an earlier digital project, so that would be our model for the look and feel of this new user interface. The work of this project, originally called the "Interface for Internet Archive," got underway in January 2011. It was publicly released as the "Theological Commons" in March 2012 with 50,000 digital texts and, as of this writing, now provides open access to over 110,000 digital items.

2 From Cataloger to Programmer: An Unexpected Career Change

At the same time as the library's partnership with the Internet Archive was starting, I made a career change on the library staff. Our first metadata librarian resigned in January 2008 and the library director encouraged me to transfer to this recently-developed position. Prior to this, I had spent eighteen years as a cataloger or manager of a cataloging unit. The transition was swift, with one of my colleagues taking on the position of acting Head Cataloger. Since the duties and work of my former position were removed, I was freed up to take on new responsibilities and, most importantly, learn a new skill set. Right from the start, Clifford Anderson, then Curator of Special Collections and also manager of the digital team, began to teach me programming using the XQuery programming language. I was now working with large groups of items in batch mode, rather than cataloging one item at a time.

There was a lead up to my transfer of roles within the library. As the Head Cataloger, I was brought in to work on a couple of early digital projects before we had a metadata librarian on staff. I also served on a metadata standards committee and was on the search committee for hiring our first metadata librarian. This activity laid the foundation for what would later—and unexpectedly—become my new role as metadata librarian. On the professional development side, in December 2006, I took a two-day training course, "Metadata Standards and Applications" designed by Diane Hillmann, a leader in this area of librarianship.

3 Learning XQuery

The XQuery programming language is a functional, declarative programming language. It was designed to query, reorganize, and transform XML data. XQuery has also been used for other programming tasks such as writing web applications; it is a general-purpose programming language specifically designed to work with XML. XQuery is considered a niche programming language and has not been widely adopted like Python or Ruby. However, its strength is that it is a powerful, expressive language perfectly suited for the work of librarians, archivists, and digital humanists who need to query, analyze, and modify their XML documents.

As a librarian trained to be a cataloger, I did not have a background in computer science. Clifford Anderson began teaching me XQuery as soon as I started working as the metadata librarian. We went over the basics of the language and he gave me the goal to write queries that would solve metadata problems: a set of queries that would function as tools for my work. That first year I was able to reach this goal as well as write my first library module of code to transform our metadata from one schema to another, which we needed to submit DOIs for journal articles. That same year digital team members and other interested library staff received three days of in-house training for XML and XQuery. Our trainer, Priscilla Walmsley, wrote the definitive book on the XQuery programming language.[2]

The key to retaining what we learned was the next step: attending and participating in weekly one-hour XQuery classes in the library. This was invaluable because we continued to learn XQuery together, sharing our newly-written queries with other staff members. This was particularly helpful to the staff members who had use cases for programming tasks in their daily work. As the metadata librarian, I had no shortage of use cases. My work gradually moved from working on metadata records by hand to accomplishing the vast majority of my work with programming.

---

[2] Priscilla Walmsley, *XQuery*, 2nd edition (Sebastopol: O'Reilly, 2016).

4 The Library's Digital Team

The library's digital team is made up of four full-time staff members. The digital team developed gradually. In the beginning, two staff members were transferred from other departments, Circulation and Cataloging. A programmer position, the Digital Library Application Developer, was added as a new position, and the digital team leader was originally the Curator of Special Collections, but later this became a separate and distinct position, the Director of Digital Initiatives. The job titles of the team members at the time of this writing are as follows: Director of Digital Initiatives; Digital Library Application Developer; Digital Production and Quality Assurance Specialist; and Metadata Librarian and XML Database Administrator.

The digital team is an agile, collaborative, and production-oriented unit. Our work methodology is called agile project management, a style of work that comes out of the software development community. Agile project management approaches, Scrum and Kanban, have been employed by the digital team to manage the processes of complex digital projects, each with a plethora of details and moving parts. We track our work on a Kanban board, a web-based tool, that is used to describe our work tasks in discreet "user stories;" we pull and work on these stories one at a time. The work is prioritized by the Director of Digital Initiatives. Tasks, notes, and attachments are added to the stories; each story is tagged with color-coded categories based on a project or task, for example, "A/V QA" or "testing." This visual tool functions as the team's central location for describing and tracking our day-to-day work. We also document our work in a wiki-style content management system, Confluence.

Another aspect of agile project management the digital team employs is the daily stand-up meeting. We meet briefly every morning to report on the work we did the day before, what problems or impediments we encountered, and what we plan to do today (based on the next assigned priority, if we have completed our current story). The Kanban board is displayed on a large monitor, so that we can refer to it. The digital team's director will sometimes capture information on the board or add a new story during the meeting. These daily meetings are a vital part of the work we do which is highly collaborative.

5 Why XML and XML Technologies?

As described so far, it is clear that the technology stack, i.e., software components, for the library's digital collections is XML and XML technologies. But why? There are other types of databases, for example, relational databases; and there are other data file formats. JSON, JavaScript Object Notation, is widely used and favored over XML by web developers in the library community.

XML stands for Extensible Markup Language. A markup language is a way to "mark up" a text so that meaningful information about the text, i.e., metadata, can be provided in tags. These tags, in the form of angle brackets, provide a human and machine-readable way of understanding the text or data.

XML was used by the library community to develop a set of rules, or schemas, for library texts and data in the early days of digital library development. These XML schemas, Dublin Core and MODS, to name only two, are well documented, maintained, and actively used by the library community.[3] Furthermore, XML technologies are also well developed and documented by the World Wide Web Consortium, commonly referred to as the W3C.[4]

6 Using a Proprietary System for Digital Collections: Benefits and Disadvantages

The library's system for digital collections is MarkLogic, a proprietary NoSQL database. It was originally designed as a native XML database. XML documents are stored natively rather than in relational database tables. There are a lot of advantages to using MarkLogic. It is designed to scale for large collections of data. It is also designed so that web applications can be quickly developed and deployed. It has a large customer base from many organizations, e.g., government, healthcare, and publishing. These are some of the benefits.

The library chose to not use an open-source system with a native XML database, although some were available. Things may have changed, but at the time the open-source options were known not to scale well. As a metadata librarian, the main downside of not using open-source software is not a technical issue, but rather more of a cultural issue. Most academic libraries favor using open-source software. Much of the professional development opportunities in the li-

---

[3] The Library of Congress, "Standards, Librarians and Archivists, Library of Congress" Accessed January 06, 2019, https://www.loc.gov/librarians/standards.
[4] World Wide Web Consortium, XML Technology, Accessed January 06, 2019, https://www.w3.org/standards/xml/.

brary community focuses on open-source systems and solutions for digital library repositories and systems.[5]

7 Working Computationally with Metadata with XML, XQuery, and XSLT

As with all digital projects, metadata plays an essential role. This interface for the Internet Archive digital content would require a lot of metadata repurposing because we already had existing metadata for the digital objects from the analog originals. The Internet Archive uses this pre-existing metadata—MARC records from the library's online catalog—to create the metadata for their user interface. We would also use the same MARC records, as MARCXML, for this purpose. Once we had the broad outline for the project, we were ready to flesh out the details. The metadata for each item would not be created by hand, but instead automatically by the repurposing of the MARCXML records. We would extract the data elements we needed using the XQuery programming language, a query language designed to work specifically with XML data. Later in the project we also used XSLT for metadata transformation. The power of XQuery allowed us to query and analyze the source metadata, i.e., assess the dataset, and also to extract and transform those data elements. We knew from our conversation with President Torrance that we would need basic descriptive data, such as author names, titles, publication dates, format, language, and subjects. We wanted to generate the subject facet assignment through automation as well. We decided we would use Library of Congress Classification numbers as our source for subjects. We took these LC class numbers and mapped them to thirty-nine subject values, for example, "Church History," "New Testament," and "Preaching," to name a few. Similarly, we would use the date values from the MARCXML record to build date facets as ranges of dates, e.g., 1851–1875. Along with the descriptive metadata, we also included the OCR text for each page of an item as part of our new XML metadata document. The OCR text would provide full-text search capabilities for users, allowing transformative search of texts by students, faculty, and library researchers, both near and far.

---

5 An active group in this area of librarianship is the Code4Lib community: https://code4lib.org/.

8 Building Metadata: Programmatic Repurposing of MARC 21 Bibliographic Records Using XQuery

The first step in the metadata process was modeling our data elements. Previously, we had used standard library metadata schemas for other digital projects. For this project, however, we decided to create a local schema which we designed based on the specific parameters of the project. At the beginning stages, we did not fully anticipate the future growth and popularity of this digital project. In hindsight, we wish we had used the library metadata schema, MODS, as it is a well-developed schema for bibliographic metadata modeled on the MARC format.[6] These are the elements we include in our local schema: id (Internet Archive identifier); name; title; sortTitle (title without initial article); uniformTitle (standardized title); edition; date; volumeInfo (wrapper element for volume and number elements); extent (wrapper element for start and end elements for journal article pages); relatedItem (wrapper element for title and sortTitle elements for journal titles); language; errorRate (percentage of errors in OCR-captured text pages); format; note; callNumber; class (subject facet); genre; series; duration; recordingDate; topics (wrapper element for individual topic elements); contributor (institution who contributed to the project); sponsor (institution that financially sponsored the digitization); marc (wrapper element for full MARC record); iaMeta (wrapper element for Internet Archive metadata XML record when there is no MARC record available); modsRecord (wrapper element for full MODS record for journal articles); and text (wrapper for page elements or transcript element for audio recording transcripts). We added elements incrementally as the project expanded to include a wider variety of material types beyond books, such as audio and video recordings, archival collections, and journal articles.

As metadata librarian, it was my responsibility to design the initial local schema. However, we now discuss and decide additional elements as a team. Each book would be represented by one metadata record, an XML document. As previously mentioned, the file would consist of both descriptive metadata and OCR text pages. We also embedded the original MARCXML record as part of the new metadata file. The embedding of the original source metadata—often referred to as legacy metadata—proved to be a providential decision. We would later enhance the new metadata with elements from this legacy data,

---

[6] At the time of this writing, the Library's digital team is in the process of mapping the Theological Commons local schema to the MODS schema.

such as edition statements, uniform titles, and series. For items that lacked a MARCXML record, we used the Internet Archive's metadata record, meta.xml, as our source metadata. We embedded these meta.xml records with our newly created metadata, as we did with the MARCXML records. Again, having the legacy metadata embedded in the new record made it easily available for future use.

We started with a small dataset of one hundred records. As previously mentioned, our database for the project is a native XML database, MarkLogic Server. For the initial test, we classified items by hand. Each Internet Archive item has a unique, persistent identifier which is very important for the metadata processing workflow, from matching to creating unique filenames. Creating the simple metadata schema and adding indexes to the system for each element was a relatively straightforward process. The real challenge came with the next task: automating the subject facet assignment.

9 Automating Subject Facet Assignment and WorldCat Search API

One of the first metadata tasks was to try to automate the subject facet assignment. In order to do this, we decided to experiment, using Library of Congress Classification, which is an alphanumeric notation. An example of an LC class number is BX4804, the class number for "Christian denominations—Protestantism—History—General works—Early through 1800." The LC class number is located in the MARC record's 050 and 090 fields. We had a problem, however, because some of our MARC bibliographic records do not contain LC call numbers. They were located in a different MARC record in our library system, the MARC holdings record. We found a solution to this problem by using the OCLC WorldCat Search API to programmatically obtain LC class numbers from the OCLC WorldCat database.[7] We extracted the first part of the author's name, usually the surname, and a portion of the title. These two values are used as parameters to search for a matching bibliographic record in the WorldCat database. For a return value we requested records that contain LC call numbers. Our programming code then extracts the first LC call number from the record, if there is at least one available. We then inserted the LC call number into our new metadata record; as a result, we were able to automate the classification for many of these unclassified items.

---

7 OCLC Developer Network, "WorldCat Search API," Accessed January 06, 2019. https://www.oclc.org/developer/develop/web-services/worldcat-search-api.en.html.

The next step to automate this process was using XQuery to query the 090/050 fields of the MARCXML records and extract the LC class number portion of the call number (a complete call number is made up of a class number, Cutter number, and date) located in the subfield coded "a." The full call number is in two subfields, but we only needed the first one, since we only needed the class portion of the LC call number. According to MARC 21 standards, use of the 090 field for local call numbers, not LC call numbers, became an obsolete practice in 1982. We discovered, unfortunately, that one of the contributing libraries was still using this 090 field for locally-defined call numbers. We will address this issue in more detail later as it caused problems with the automated workflow.

Once we had the LC class number, we wrote XQuery code that mapped the class number to a subject facet value. The subject facets are based on the Library of Congress Classification with some minor modifications. Because we were using only thirty-nine subjects, for many of the classes we only needed the alphabetic part of the class number. So, LC class "B" was mapped to "Philosophy" and "BT" to "Theology." Some alphanumeric class numbers were also used to divide class number ranges into more granular subject areas, e.g., BV class numbers were broken out based on the numeric portion of the class numbers to map to several subject values: "Worship," "Ecclesiology," "Missions," "Practical Theology," and "Preaching."

Finally, we were left with some items that lacked an LC class number in the MARCXML record and that also did not obtain one from the OCLC WorldCat Search API query. For these items we classified them by hand using a web-based classification tool designed by our programmer. Generally, there is some manual work that is needed to complete the descriptive metadata process. A great deal can be automated, but not everything. Using programming for the majority of the work is optimal and should always be considered the first method in a metadata workflow for large datasets.

10 Data Cleaning: Problematic Classification Metadata

As previously mentioned, one of the contributing libraries whose books we imported into the Theological Commons continued to use an obsolete practice when classifying items; they used the 090 field for a local classification system. The 090 field is now reserved for LC classification call numbers only. As a result, our automated process broke down for these items. The alphabetic part of their classification meant something completely different from LC classification. When metadata standards are not followed, semantic chaos ensues! We encountered the same problem with a portion of our bibliographic records for special collection materials; some of the local "SC call numbers" were put in the 090 field instead of the 099 field. The 099 field is the correct field for call numbers based on a local system, not LC classification. Fortunately, we were able to programmatically identify, isolate, and classify these outlier items, bypassing the regular mapping and using the OCLC WorldCat API instead.

11 Data Cleaning: Normalizing Metadata

Another metadata task that was important to the early development of this project was normalization of metadata used for sorting search results, specifically author names and titles. We set up a separate namespace, a named element set, in the local schema called "sort" to create XML elements <sort:creator> and <sort:title>. We used Regular Expressions, a pattern-matching programming language, to remove initial articles and punctuation to create title values to sort on or to format a name to sort on a surname when present.

12 Metadata Enrichment through Computational Processes: Editions, Series, Uniform Titles, and Volume Information

After the metadata schema and import process was completed, the next step for metadata work was enriching or enhancing the metadata by adding other fields to the descriptive metadata. As mentioned earlier, we retained a copy of the original metadata embedded in our new metadata record. For this next step, we queried this legacy metadata and extracted fields that we did not use previously. We wanted to provide richer, more robust metadata to our users. For example, the uniform title is a standardized title that brings together the same work published under different titles. An example of a standardized title in the Theological Commons is "Augsburg Confession." If the user clicks on this title, the results are two books, "The Augsburg Confession" and "Extract of the twenty-one doctrinal articles of the Augustan or Augsburg Confession."

One of the interesting, and challenging, side effects of digitization is the atomization of multi-volume book sets. In the physical realm, the user finds the multi-volume book sets together on the library's shelves, and often described as a unit in the library catalog. In the digital realm, however, each volume is digitized separately and it is up to the user to track down all the volumes. We wanted to bring these multi-volume sets back together in the user interface—to facilitate this discovery process for the user. This was another metadata task that started with programming followed by manual editing.

Using the XQuery programming language, we located duplicate titles that included volume information in the 300 field of the MARC record. We added the volume information to our new metadata and created an id attribute, a portion of the Internet Archive identifier, which was added to the <volumeInfo> element. This id attribute was used under the hood, so to speak, in the user interface to provide a way to group together all the volumes of a set (actually all the volumes of a specific title). If the user clicks on the link, "View all volumes," the resulting set is all the volumes of a specific title.

In my role as metadata librarian, I programmatically generated reports for each directory in the Theological Commons database. The reports contained lists of titles. These titles represented duplicate titles with multiple volumes. The lists were used by staff and student workers for the manual editing process, necessitated by the fact that accurate volume, issue, and part information require human review and editing. The work was done in the metadata editor tool by copying and pasting in each title and verifying the item and its volume designation, since the editor tool allows for viewing both the metadata and digitized item.

This volume procedure was added to the import process so that the volume information could be captured at the point of ingest when the new metadata documents are created. Subsequently, staff checked and edited that information in the editor tool.

13 Content Selection: Identifying Texts Manually and Programmatically

At the end of October 2011, we were ready to scale up the project by importing not only our contributions to the Internet Archive, but also adding items from other libraries within the scope of religion and theology. Our goal was to load a total of 50,000 digital books before launching the new user interface live to the public. This was a two-pronged workflow. Our programmer was tasked with developing an automated method to add books to the database based on religion and theology LC subject headings. At the same time, our production specialist and I were tasked with putting into place the manual workflow. I trained five members of the library staff to import books manually based on keywords in religion and theology. Like the manual classification process, we had developed a web-based import tool that the staff would use for this part of the project. One of the important aspects of using web-based tools is that they allow the human editors to focus on content entry and avoid dealing with the detailed complexity of XML markup.

14 Metadata Analysis and Assessment

One of the processes that metadata librarians share with digital humanists is metadata analysis or assessment. For digital humanists, their reasons for analysis are more of a research focus; for metadata librarians, we tend to focus more on assessment. We need to assess the quality of metadata, for instance. Putting aside the differences, our computational approaches and tools may be very similar. My tool of choice is the XQuery programming language. This powerful, expressive query language provides the ability to navigate XML data, isolate different parts of an XML document, and return results in a way that allows for disparate parts to come together to be counted, analyzed, and compared, to name just a few of the possibilities. Another important tool for metadata work is the programming language XSLT. XSLT was designed specifically to transform XML documents.

15 Expansion of Project Scope: Adding Non-Print Audiovisual Items

In December 2013, I began a new phase of metadata work for the Theological Commons: adding audio and video content from the seminary's Educational Media collection. This phase of the Theological Commons development illustrates the process of bringing together and repurposing metadata from multiple, disparate sources. We had created brief MARC records for approximately six thousand audio recordings and loaded them into the library's catalog. That was one source of metadata. I also gained access to the Educational Media's internal spreadsheets which captured metadata for audio and video metadata at the time the recordings were being made.

The first step was to programmatically extract the MARC records, as MARCXML, from the library catalog. I accomplished this using a Representational State Transfer API or RESTful API, part of the library's systems web services. I created a separate, temporary database to be used for the purpose of creating new metadata records for this project.

The second step was to extract the spreadsheet metadata and transform it into MARCXML records. This was done with a popular library cataloging tool called MarcEdit. Once the spreadsheet metadata was in MARCXML format, I was able to compare the two sets of records, the ones from the library catalog and the ones from the spreadsheet, by comparing identifiers and removing duplicates.

16 Conclusion: Library Digital Projects and How They Can Transform Theological Scholarship

It has already been suggested that digitizing and providing full-text search has transformed how library users can find and interact with texts. While the quality of OCR text varies, it is still an incredible feat to be able to do keyword searches across large datasets of items that used to be only accessible in print form. Just this act of digitization can transform how scholars of theology interact with texts. Full-text search also opens the doors to finding relationships among both textual and non-textual resources that might not have been noticed in their original analog forms. Besides full text, this is also due to the more granular item-level metadata that is often provided for digitized items; the digitization of archival collections of manuscripts is a good example of this change. Deeper and more analytical forms of text analysis are made possible as well since the Internet Archive provides ways to download both text and metadata files for reuse. Scholars can analyze text in their own programming environment, conducting, for example, statistical analysis with the Python or R programming languages.

Another transformation that we have noticed in the development of these digital projects is their capability to extend the use of these formerly analog items in an international context. The Internet has provided a means to share knowledge from our library to others studying theology across the world. Digitization has also helped to facilitate collaborative projects, a sharing of tools and expertise in countries outside the United States. This is another way that theological scholarship is being transformed by this significant effort within the theological library community.

III Digital Humanities Pedagogy

Richard Manly Adams, Jr.
Defining Digital Pedagogy in Theological Libraries

Libraries are, at their best, institutions that teach. I often get confused looks when I describe to non-librarians what I do. It seems the general public thinks about librarians as curators and collectors, and so when I talk about how much of my work (and that of my colleagues) involves instruction, whether in a classroom, in a workshop, or at a reference desk, people are surprised. Librarians are teachers; I tend to emphasize Atla's identification of us as "connectors," for I think that holds true for what each of us do. We connect our patrons, be they faculty, students, or staff, with the resources and skills that they need to succeed.

In a digital age, though, just how a library and its librarians implement that instructional identity has come into question. The introduction of new tools, of new sources of information, and of new avenues for scholarly output creates an opportunity for libraries to reassert their essential role in the teaching mission of many theological schools, but the library will only be successful in reasserting this role if librarians carefully consider how teaching must be adapted to the new norms of a digital age. The question in this chapter is how libraries can maintain their instructional identity when the needs of our patrons and the possibilities for scholarly output are changing so quickly.

1 Attempts to Define Digital Pedagogy

Consideration of how libraries must adapt instruction in a digital age must begin with the popular term "digital pedagogy." The digital age has introduced us to new and often vague concepts like "digital pedagogy." New ideas are often followed by battles over defining new terms. Consider, for example, the world of scholarship focused on defining the concept "digital humanities." In the minds of many, definitions of that term have become so varied that the term lacks any helpful meaning, not to mention attempts to define the many cognate terms such as "digital scholarship" or "humanities computing."[1] Perhaps sur-

---

[1] For discussions of the history of defining this term, see Matthew G. Kirschenbaum, "What Is Digital Humanities and What's It Doing in English Departments?," *ADE Bulletin*.150 (2010): 1–7. Melissa Terras, Julianne Nyhan, and Edward Vanhoutte, eds., *Defining Digital Humanities: A*

OpenAccess. © 2021 Richard Manly Adams, Jr., published by De Gruyter. This work is licensed under the Creative Commons Attribution-NonCommercial-NoDerivatives 4.0 International License.
https://doi.org/10.1515/9783110536539-008

prisingly, though, a definition of the equally-significant term "digital pedagogy" has not been considered as thoroughly. Within recent consideration, emphasis has fallen on each word, with some emphasizing digital pedagogy as a shift in instructional method, while others reading it as a shift in instructional content. The first group emphasizes *pedagogy*, reading "digital pedagogy" to describe approaches to teaching that incorporate digital methods and tools in the delivery of content. For example, Brian Croxall has defined digital pedagogy as "the use of electronic elements to enhance or to change the experience of education."[2] Croxall provides examples of digital pedagogy that range from the use of PowerPoint in the classroom to the teaching of massive open online courses (MOOCs). Understood in this way, digital pedagogy means enhancing teaching through the incorporation of digital tools or pedagogical methods made possible through digital technologies. To engage in "digital pedagogy" is to deliver instruction by implementing new digital tools. Under this definition falls the "flipped classroom" and online instruction, as well as the use of videos to deliver instruction or the incorporation of digital exhibits or text mining tools into course assignments.

Operating under this definition, many librarians continue in a traditional instructional support role. That is, participating in "digital pedagogy," the librarian works to convince and aid those who serve in traditional teaching roles to integrate new digital tools into content delivery in the classroom. Librarian support may come in the form of electronic course reserves, managing or training on a school's learning management system, or teaching faculty best practices in online and hybrid course delivery. Studies have shown that through the incorporation of digital tools, students can be more engaged, content can be more effectively delivered, and schools can expand and diversify their student bodies.[3] Therefore, under this definition, librarians interested in digital pedagogy should ask how they can encourage faculty to incorporate new tools and methods to enhance the classroom experience.

Reader (Surrey: Ashgate, 2013). David M. Berry and Anders Fagerjord, *Digital Humanities: Knowledge and Critique in a Digital Age* (Cambridge, UK: Polity Press, 2017).

2 Brian Croxall, "'Digital Pedagogy'?," *A Digital Pedagogy Unconference*, August 30, 2012, http://www.briancroxall.net/digitalpedagogy/what-is-digital-pedagogy/. For a similar understanding of the term digital pedagogy, see Myra Waddell and Elena Clariza, "Critical Digital Pedagogy and Cultural Sensitivity in the Library Classroom: Infographics and Digital Storytelling," *College & Research Libraries News* 79.5 (2018): 228–32.

3 For examples of studies highlighting the benefits of integrating digital tools into traditional courses, see Deborah Tritt and Carie Heatherly, "Practitioners as Professors: Experiential Learning in the Distance Digital Liberal Arts Classroom," *College & Undergraduate Libraries* 24.2–4 (2017): 545–58. Hannah Jacobs, "Collaborative Teaching and Digital Visualization in an Art History Classroom," *Visual Resources Association Bulletin* 43.2 (2016): 1–11.

As opposed to that instrumentalist view of "digital pedagogy," where the digital enhances the mode of instructional delivery, some have defined "digital pedagogy" by emphasizing new content as the focus of instruction. That is, some understand the *digital* as the object of the pedagogy, enacting "digital pedagogy" as equipping students to live, work, and produce scholarship in a digital age. In this mode, an instructor shifts his or her focus to teach the skills and methods popular in the digital age so as to prepare students to live and work in a world that is defined not only by new tools, but by new modes of thinking, reading, and communicating. Methods of teaching with this understanding may range from direct instruction in digital tools to opening the possibility of digital humanities projects as student output. Stewart Varner understands "digital pedagogy" in this way when he notes, "Librarians would do well to expand their concept of instruction to include the ability to find, evaluate, and learn to use new tools for exploring, sharing, reusing, and remixing research materials."[4]

Operating with this definition, the librarian is often in a more direct teaching mode, as the instruction on digital tools and methods is often viewed as paracurricular. A school or program must continue to deliver its traditional content, and so the library is asked to supplement course offerings with workshops designed to teach students the skills and tools to succeed in a digital age. The librarian, therefore, is invited to see his or her job to be the facilitating of the introduction of new tools into the classroom, allowing instructors to teach their students in new ways.

Readers will likely agree on the import of both understandings of "digital pedagogy." Librarians should certainly not be forced into choosing one or the other, and instead should embrace both new methods of teaching and new content to be taught as an opportunity to increase their impact on campus. In this essay, though, I try to hold these two together by arguing that digital pedagogy should not be limited by defining it in either way. That is, I emphasize how libraries can introduce digital tools to enhance the teaching that is happening at our institutions, and at the same time encourage librarians to train patrons who are more equipped to operate in a digital world.

Librarians need to think about how we are teaching and what outcomes we are looking for, before we focus on the specific tools we are introducing. My argument is in line with Paul Fyfe's concern that, "Perhaps the most common short-

---

[4] Stewart Varner, "Library Instruction for Digital Humanities Pedagogy in Undergraduate Classes," *Laying the Foundation: Digital Humanities in Academic Libraries*, ed. John W. White and Heather Gilbert (West Lafayette, IN: Purdue University Press, 2016).

coming of digital pedagogy is how frequently it gets conceived in terms of instructional technology."[5] Likewise, Jesse Stommel argues, "Digital pedagogy is an orientation toward pedagogy that does not fetishize digital tools."[6] Like so many other aspects of our approach to the digital age, we librarians in our instruction run the risk of taking an instrumentalist view of technology, of equating the changes in our digital age with the introduction of the electronic tools that surround us.

My central argument is that libraries have an essential role to play in digital pedagogy, and that role goes far beyond introducing students and faculty to the latest tools. Rather, libraries must see their mission as developing patrons' skills to think critically about what new tools, ideas, and methods are doing to communication and how we can best take advantage of them to maximize impact.

2 The Danger of the Status Quo

To make this argument about the library's role in digital pedagogy, I begin in a descriptive mode, considering how libraries are currently teaching in the digital age. In looking at the literature about digital pedagogy and libraries, I find much that concerns me about the way libraries have entered the digital age in terms of their teaching.

John Russell and Merinda Kaye Hensley, in a December 2017 piece in *College and Research Libraries News*, capture well my concern about how librarians have approached teaching tools and methods for the digital humanities. Russell and Hensley warn against a focus on "buttonology," a term they define as follows: "There is a danger with digital humanities instruction of falling into the trap of buttonology. By buttonology, we do not mean the study of buttons. . . . Buttonology is, in its simplest terms, software training that surveys different features of an interface in an introductory manner."[7] Many librarians likely recognize a "buttonology" approach to the teaching or learning of digital humanities. Most have been invited to or attended countless Voyant or StoryMap JS sessions offered in libraries, sessions which emphasize how to use this or that particular tool, but with little focus on the context for why the tool is needed, the practical problem

---

[5] Paul Fyfe, "Digital Pedagogy Unplugged," DHQ 5:3 (2011), http://www.digitalhumanities.org/dhq/vol/5/3/000106/000106.html.
[6] https://www.tiki-toki.com/timeline/entry/392826/Digital-Pedagogy-a-Genealogy/
[7] John E. Russell and Merinda Kaye Hensley, "Beyond Buttonology: Digital Humanities, Digital Pedagogy, and the ACRL Framework," *College and Research Libraries News* 78.11 (2017): 588.

that one might use the tool to solve, and how engagement in scholarship on a digital platform creates new opportunities and challenges.

Russell and Hensley continue by noting that library literature on digital humanities pedagogy tends to be "practical, with a focus on how best to present digital tools."[8] A quick search of the library literature, particularly in the field of theological librarianship, confirms this, with reports of workshops and instructional sessions seemingly designed to give users a crash course in this particular tool or the next.

I do not here offer a blanket critique of workshops as a form of library instruction, even workshops on digital tools. I work in a library that offers dozens of instructional sessions on a range of tools, such as Accordance, Zotero, Voyant, and StoryMap, and these are very effective ways to open students' eyes to new capacities for research and communication in a digital age. Where else are students going to learn these new tools that are going to be essential in their future work?

However, I share the critique of the buttonology approach to the digital humanities in library instruction if these workshops are librarians' singular attempts at instruction in a digital age. Such a limited approach to digital pedagogy represents a missed opportunity for libraries, but more importantly it falls short of teaching our patrons what they need in order to succeed in the digital world. I find flawed an approach that begins by outlining the use of a tool, assuming a student will place this tool in his or her toolkit and eventually find a problem that the tool solves. All of our patrons face an overload of new ideas, concepts, and methods, and the library's buttonology approach simply places the new tool, even something as helpful as Voyant, as one more thing to learn.

A close parallel to this buttonology approach to digital tools, one which I also find flawed, is books that introduce various modes of biblical exegesis, without first introducing the problems these methods of exegesis seek to answer. Consider, for example, the organization of one popular exegesis book into separate chapters that identify one mode of criticism after another.[9] First a student learns of textual criticism, then form criticism, then redaction criticism. Multiple modes of taking apart a text are presented to the student as a range of options for how one can get started with writing an exegesis paper. What is missing, though, is an introduction to the problems in the biblical texts that these different modes of exegesis sought to answer when they were first introduced. The reader is never

---

8 Russell and Hensley, "Beyond Buttonology," 588.
9 See John H. Hayes and Carl R. Holladay, *Biblical Exegesis: A Beginner's Handbook*, 3rd Edition (Louisville: Westminster John Knox Press, 2007).

invited to consider, for example, that Rudolf Bultmann did not engage in form criticism because it was the particular method he learned about in a workshop. Rather, he engaged in form criticism because he started to recognize a basic pattern in the pronouncement stories in Matthew's gospel and was curious how these might have developed and what their development might tell us about earliest Christianity.

In a similar way, I often find introductions to various tools used by digital humanists to be an ineffective way of introducing our patrons, be they students or faculty, to the power of new methods of scholarship. The challenge of this buttonology approach to teaching the digital humanities is that our patrons may not yet have problems to which these tools are offered as solutions. This buttonology approach, understanding digital instruction as equipping students with tools to eventually employ, is a first problem I identify with what we have been doing in our workshop approach to the tools of digital humanities. We offer solutions to problems that our patrons have not yet identified.

There is a second, and in many ways deeper, problem with a workshop approach to the tools of digital humanities. Typical approaches to digital pedagogy reflect an instrumentalist view of technology, one which has been identified as problematic at least since the early twentieth century and the work of key philosophers of technology, notably Martin Heidegger.[10] A buttonology approach would suggest that the digital age has gifted us with some new ways of doing scholarship, and all one needs to do is learn the new tools. So, while a key example of scholarly output was previously a twenty-page exegetical essay, it is now an audio/visual timeline constructed online. With such an approach, we offer students no space to reflect critically on how new tools change our scholarly communities, what opportunities they open up for reaching new audiences, and the problems, be they ethical or practical, the use of such tools might create.

To this point, my argument has largely been a negative one—critiquing what I find lacking in librarians' approaches to digital pedagogy. What solutions do I offer? I do not intend to suggest there is a single silver bullet for how libraries should approach the introduction of the digital age to the classroom. I do, however, offer a few guiding principles, with some examples of how they have been implemented, as an opening for a conversation about what critical digital peda-

---

10 See Martin Heidegger, "The Question Concerning Technology," in *Basic Writings*, Revised, Expanded Edition, Harper Perennial Modern Thought (New York: Harper Collins, 2008), 307–41. For expanded analysis, see Ivan Illich, *In the Vineyard of the Text: A Commentary to Hugh's Didascalicon* (Chicago: University of Chicago Press, 1996); Elaine Graham, "Being, Making and Imagining: Toward a Practical Theology of Technology," *Culture and Religion* 10.2 (2009): 221–36.

gogy might look like in the theological library. I briefly introduce these here in hopes that they are generative of reflection for you in others' particular contexts.

3 All Library Instruction Should Combine the Practical with the Reflective

The idea that tools are not neutral, and thus the adoption of new tools creates the potential for introducing new bias, is something we all likely recognize inherently. However, the ubiquity of digital tools in our daily lives demands that libraries equip students to think critically about who is controlling our information and what role we are playing in the information ecology. If we simply lay more tools at our patrons' feet, we become part of the problem rather than the solution. For example, I often ask my students to tell me why the Waze app on their phone invites them to turn left rather than turn right on their way to a destination, and they are often dumbfounded to even consider this as a question. The "why" behind an algorithm is not a natural question to my students.[11] As librarians, therefore, when we introduce even more digital tools into our patrons' lives, we carry the obligation to start these conversations about the complex tradeoffs between convenience and privacy that we make every day.

The ACRL Framework for Information Literacy is a helpful model for introducing such a critical element into our digital pedagogy.[12] Just as the framework encourages librarians to train students to recognize that authority in bibliographic sources is constructed and contextual, so we must train students that their adoption of various tools is not a neutral act and will likely have unintended consequences for their scholarship, their community, or their congregations. The convenience and power of digital tools, facts that are so often the focus of the buttonology approach to teaching digital tools, come with many downsides, and it is our job to ensure that our students have considered the tradeoffs they are making when choosing new tools. While patrons may benefit from the convenience of using a service like MailChimp to maintain a mailing list and facilitate mass communication, they are also exposing themselves to the vulnerability of trusting an unknown vendor with securing the privacy of those with whom they communicate. If we as librarians do not invite students to recognize this

---

11 There have been a number of important works analyzing the biases built into the algorithms of our ubiquitous digital tools. For a supreme example, see Safiya Noble, *Algorithms of Oppression: How Search Engines Reinforce Racism* (New York: NYU Press, 2018).
12 http://www.ala.org/acrl/standards/ilframework.

tradeoff, we not only fail to live up to the standards of the framework, but we have not truly taught our patrons to thrive in a digital age.

Fortunately, many of us work and are trained in a discipline that has thousands of years of examples of engagement with technology. Much as our students may think the challenges of the digital age are new, church history is screaming with examples of adapting to new tools and methods. I often use the example of the broadcast of sermons on the radio in the early twentieth century. Sermon broadcasts were initially quite successful in the white church, but less so in the black church. Jonathan Walton, in his book *Watch This*, documenting the history of black televangelism, offers an explanation: "The first preacher recorded on a major label was Rev. Calvin P. Dixon in 1925. Columbia [Records]'s race series inaugural religious effort, however, did not make a great splash among targeted consumers.... The sole emphasis was on Dixon's sermon, yet a preacher constitutes only one part of the Du Boisian descriptive trinity of 'the Preacher, the Music and the Frenzy.'"[13] The shift in medium changed the message, and the church had to adapt its use of the growing technology in order to best meet its goals. This analysis is the type of critical engagement for which our students must be equipped. Just as Walton's analysis suggests that the church would not have been well-served by generic introductions to the use of the radio to disseminate sermons, so our patrons are not well-served by workshops simply introducing them to new possibilities offered by digital tools. Rather, they need to be challenged to recognize that their adoption of new tools is not a neutral act, but rather new tools will by definition change the way they communicate to particular audiences. My concern is that the space for this type of reflection on this rarely exists for our students; I see this as a primary role for digital pedagogy in the library. We must introduce the tools, but we must also invite students to see them as more than tools.

4 Digital Pedagogy Must Be Deeply Integrated into the Existing Classroom

As noted above, one of the challenges with a buttonology approach to digital pedagogy is the extra-curricular nature of how it often happens. Often, we inundate our students with the possibilities of various tools, rather than offering the tools as a solution to the specific problem they are seeking to answer.

---

[13] Jonathan L. Walton, *Watch This! The Ethics and Aesthetics of Black Televangelism* (New York: NYU Press, 2009), 34.

One remedy to this challenge is to introduce tools and methods within the space of a classroom and replace, rather than add to, what students are asked to do. At my library, we have had great success by working with faculty to replace the traditional exegesis paper, for example, with a digital exhibition or Wikipedia edit, inviting students to take the problem they are already working on and to see the digital tool or method as a way of addressing it. The just-in-time nature of instruction on new tools is essential to grow their adoption rate, and it invites in students the necessary curiosity of asking what other digital tools might be out there. And as we all know, the effective teacher is not the one who effectively trains in some method or tool, but rather the one who sparks the imagination in the student to ask what else is out there.

5 Successful Digital Pedagogy Equips as Well as Instructs

Alongside meeting students with digital solutions for problems they are already asking, successful digital pedagogy supports students by helping them tear down the barriers to entry in creating digital projects. These barriers can be technical and knowledge-based, but they can often also be financial. Instruction without a path toward implementation is bound to fail.

We realized this problem at my library quickly when we offered workshops on the creation and curation of one's digital presence. We offered (in my mind) excellent instruction on how to build a WordPress site, but once students realized that they needed to invest some of their money in order to have full access to the range of tools wordpress.org offered, then they quickly forgot what they were learning. We sought to remedy this by introducing a Domain of One's Own program. Here we not only encourage students to develop a web-based project to promote their scholarship or their nonprofit or whatever, but we also provide them server space, a URL, and a set number of hours of consulting to get them started, at a small cost to the library, a cost that would be prohibitive for many of our students.

The barrier may not always be financial. It may be that students are lacking certain technical skills, vocabulary, or experience to increase adoption, and the library can play a role in guiding them toward collaboration partners or introducing them to training opportunities. The point is simply that the library cannot see its pedagogical role to end with the moment of instruction. Rather, the library must equip its patrons to succeed with their implementation of the digital, not merely understanding its pedagogical role to end with the introduction or exposure to new tools.

6 We Must Partner Digital Pedagogy with Digital Scholarship in the Library

The methods and skills of digital scholarship are difficult to teach in a vacuum, that is without real life examples. Fortunately for us, we all work in libraries, which are themselves platforms for implementing digital approaches and tools. Gone are the days when one could stand by the saying "those who can't do, teach." Methods in digital scholarship demand practitioners be the ones who teach, and they demand opportunities for students who want to put to work what they have learned.

In our library, we have had great success with marrying the instruction of new methods or tools with work opportunities for students to develop those tools based on digital projects ongoing in the library. For example, we have built a Howard Thurman digital audio archive, a project that involves learning digital exhibitions, graphic design, metadata curation, GIS mapping, transcription, etc.[14] The project has been built not merely by external contractors and library staff, but also with significant support from our student patrons. What better way to teach these skills than to invite students to participate in a project, to learn on the job, and in turn to benefit the library (and build a CV line)? The more libraries can connect an actual output of digital scholarship with digital pedagogy, the more successful they will be.

7 A Better Way Forward

I close with a return to the question of definition of the term "digital pedagogy." Is it using digital tools to teach, or is it teaching digital tools? I hope that you see that I believe it is both. That is, "digital pedagogy" means opening up patrons' minds to the power of the tools and methods of the digital age, sparking their creativity to critically engage this digital world in their learning and their creating. The outcome may be that patrons are emboldened to use digital tools in their scholarship or their teaching, or it may be that they take a more careful and critical approach to the digital tools that surround them. Either way, our job as li-

---

14 See http://thurman.pitts.emory.edu.

brarians engaged in digital pedagogy is to introduce patrons to a new mode of critical thinking, open to the introduction of new tools, supported with the resources to learn to use them, and cognizant of the implications the adoption of these tools may have.

Why should we introduce digital pedagogy into our library instruction? I emphasize to my colleagues that digital pedagogy is not simply an opportunity for the library to find something to do, to show its value to the institution. Rather, I find it to be a moral obligation, to ensure our students can enter into this digital age equipped not only to build things like websites, but also to think critically about how their building may impact their work. Most of my students are M.Div.s, often on the younger end of the scale. I imagine (and have heard) that she is going to walk into her first congregational call with all eyes upon her as the "young person" who by default is asked to rebuild the church website, manage the live streaming, and oversee social media. My goal in teaching is not only to equip her with the skills she needs to do those things and the places to go to learn what she doesn't know, but also to embolden her to think carefully about why the church may or may not need these tools and what impact they will have on her ministry.

The role of critical digital pedagogy is essential, and I fear that if the library isn't going to do it, it isn't going to be done.

Clifford B. Anderson and Gayathri Narasimham
An Introduction to the Beauty and Joy of Computing for Theological Librarians

The dizzying growth of the digital humanities during the past decade has kindled interest among students and faculty at divinity schools and theological seminaries in technologies such as markup languages, geospatial information systems, and network analysis applications.[1] This growth has likewise sparked the curiosity of theological librarians in supporting teaching and research in the digital humanities. Indicative of this interest are the recurring presentations about the digital humanities at Atla annual meetings and webinars.[2] As theological schools prepare students for careers in the church and social ministries, is there a way to provide them with a humanistic and theological perspective on our increasingly computational and algorithmically-driven society? The COVID-19 pandemic has reinforced the need for understanding of the digital world, as pastors seek to communicate with their congregations using tools like Zoom, Facebook, and the Adobe Creative Cloud, and as they worry about the distorting effects of filter bubbles, echo chambers, and the digital divide on their church members.

The teaching of digital humanities at theological institutions raises distinct challenges, however. At university-based divinity schools, students and faculty may discover like-minded colleagues at digital humanities centers or digital scholarship labs. But the staff members in these digital scholarship units may not have expertise in religious studies or theology. At independent theological schools, by contrast, the task of teaching digital humanities may fall to intrepid

---

[1] An initial version of this paper was presented at Snap!Con 2020 on July 31, 2020 (see Clifford Anderson and Gayathri Narasimham, "Teaching BJC with NetsBlox," Short Talk, [July 2020]). The authors would also like to thank David Michelson and Mark Schoenfeld for their comments and suggestions for improvements on prior drafts of this paper.
[2] Clifford B. Anderson, Christopher P. Benda, and Eileen Crawford, "Doing Digital Humanities in Theological Libraries," in *American Theological Library Association Summary of Proceedings*, vol. 69, 2015, 189–97; Bobby Smiley, "Theological Librarianship in the Age of Digital Humanities," ed. Tawney Burgess, *Summary of Proceedings, 70th Annual Conference of the American Theological Library Association*, vol. 70, 2016, 22–32; Richard Manly Jr. Adams et al., "Digital Humanities and Libraries and Archives in Religious Studies," in *American Theological Library Association Summary of Proceedings*, vol. 73, 2019, 42–48; Richard Manly Jr. Adams and Clifford B Anderson, "Digital Humanities and Libraries and Archives in Religious Studies," Webinar (November 2020), https://vimeo.com/480835487.

OpenAccess. © 2021 Clifford B. Anderson and Gayathri Narasimham, published by De Gruyter.
This work is licensed under the Creative Commons Attribution-NonCommercial-NoDerivatives 4.0 International License. https://doi.org/10.1515/9783110536539-009

faculty or librarians who, having taught themselves, have learned enough to offer workshops or experimental courses in digital humanities.

We argue that the best way to prepare students for ministry in an increasingly computational context is to teach the fundamentals of computational thinking and algorithmic literacy rather than specific tools and techniques, which arise and fade away at an accelerating pace. We believe that theological librarians may learn from the innovators of the *Beauty and Joy of Computing* (https://bjc.berkeley.edu/) curriculum about how to provide these foundations to students, either in collaboration with faculty or as co-curricular library instruction in digital literacy. In this paper, we discuss the origin and implementation of a BJC course at Vanderbilt University as well as subsequent efforts to adapt its core ideas to teaching the digital humanities.

1 Collaborators

Clifford B. Anderson approaches the teaching of digital humanities primarily from the perspective of librarianship and theological studies. Anderson is a librarian who also holds a secondary appointment as professor of religious studies. Over the past decade, he has taught digital humanists, primarily from disciplines like English or history but also foreign languages and theology, among others, to write programs to address questions in their disciplines. Given his interest in digital editions in the Text Encoding Initiative (TEI), Anderson's primary programming language is XQuery, a functional programming language for processing XML and JSON.[3] For several years, he ran a weekly seminar on XQuery at the Vanderbilt University Libraries.

Gayathri Narasimham has a background in psychology and digital learning. She has taught courses in statistics and research methods and more recently organized a workshop in data visualization. She has programming experience in Python and R, and wanted to explore teaching a first-level, introductory computer science course for undergraduates who did not have a background in CS or coding. In addition, Narasimham also teaches sections of the required ethics course for undergraduate computer science majors.

The authors adapted the course from curriculum developed at the University of California, Berkeley as well as from its implementation at the high school level

---

[3] See Clifford B. Anderson and Joseph C. Wicentowski, *XQuery for Digital Humanists* (College Station: Texas A&M University Press, 2020).

to teach AP CS Principles.[4] While seeking to stay true to the vision of the BJC, we tailored the course to fit our academic schedule, meet the needs of our undergraduates, and expand the range of programming concepts we taught. This experience leads us to believe that the principles of the BJC, suitably adjusted, might become a vehicle for teaching computational thinking or algorithmic literacy to students and scholars of religious studies and theology. In this paper, we discuss the difficulty of provisioning instruction in the digital humanities to students of religion and theology and suggest why customizing the BJC and a blocks-based environment would go a long way toward meeting those pedagogical challenges.

2 Challenges with Teaching Coding in the Digital Humanities

The question whether there is an intrinsic connection between computer programming and digital humanities has turned out to be fraught. While, as Bethany Nowviskie reminds us, the so-called 'hack' versus 'yack' (or coding versus theorizing) debate may have turned out to be a straw person argument all along,[5] the question of how much programming students of the digital humanities should learn in the course of their studies remains a live issue.

If you plan to teach students to program as part of a digital humanities course, to what degree should you contextualize that instruction? This question surfaces across many disciplines. As computation becomes increasingly intrinsic to many disciplines, ranging from computational biology to computational musicology and beyond, instructors grapple with the best way to integrate programming skills within disciplinary courses. As Mark Guzdial has noted, contextualizing computer science education promotes student engagement and retention, but at some cost to instructional efficiency and transferability of knowledge between domains.[6]

---

4 Daniel D. Garcia, Brian Harvey, and Luke Segars, "CS Principles Pilot at University of California, Berkeley," *ACM Inroads* 3, no. 2 (June 2012): 58–60, doi:10.1145/2189835.2189853.
5 Bethany Nowviskie, "On the Origin of 'Hack' and 'Yack,'" in *Debates in the Digital Humanities 2016*, ed. Matthew K. Gold and Lauren F. Klein (Minneapolis: University of Minnesota Press, 2016), 66–70, doi:10.5749/j.ctt1cn6thb.10.
6 Mark Guzdial, "Does Contextualized Computing Education Help?" *ACM Inroads* 1, no. 4 (December 2010): 4–6, doi:10.1145/1869746.1869747.

A ready-to-hand solution is complementing a major with a minor or major in computer science.[7] For students who are motivated to learn computer science in its own right, undertaking a double major or adding a minor is a possibility, though it leaves students with the task of integrating the disciplines. As data science emerges as an independent interdisciplinary field of study, students from quantitively-focused disciplines may benefit from adding a minor in data science since the connections are already latent. But, as Susan Mitchell and Katharine Cole observe, for students from other disciplines such as the humanities, fulfilling the mathematical prerequisites may prove challenging and, in general, they may also find few areas of overlap between the courses in their majors.[8] An alternative is to develop a CS+X program, which aims to teach computer science from the perspective of particular disciplines.

David J. Birnbaum and Alison Langmead make the case for what they term "a task-driven programming pedagogy" when teaching digital humanists to program.[9] Drawing inspiration from contemporary trends in foreign language instruction, they contend that the emphasis in programming instruction should be on accomplishing goals relevant to the digital humanities, not trying to master the syntax and grammar of a computing language encyclopedically (at least not at first).

> But, just as in the case of the movement away from a grammatical focus in language teaching to an oral-proficiency focus, there is another type of programming textbook and another type of course: the task-based, proficiency-oriented one. Books of this sort sometimes include the word "cookbook" in the title, and what characterizes these books (and courses that follow the same model) is that they are organized not around learning, say, all of the numeric data types and then all of the non-numeric simple types and then all of the complex types, but around accomplishing specific coding tasks.[10]

The approach they counsel is to remain agile, approximating the practices of digital humanities practitioners by learning how to break up big conceptual problems into smaller executable tasks ("algorithmic thinking"), relying on second-

---

[7] Susan Mitchell and Katharine Cole, "X+CS: A Computing Pathway for Non-Computer Science Majors," American Society for Engineering Education, in *ASEE Mid Atlantic Section Spring Conference*, 2020), 3

[8] Ibid.

[9] David J. Birnbaum and Alison Langmead, "Task-Driven Programming Pedagogy in the Digital Humanities," in *New Directions for Computing Education: Embedding Computing Across Disciplines*, ed. Samuel B. Fee, Amanda M. Holland-Minkley, and Thomas E. Lombardi (Cham: Springer International Publishing, 2017), 63–85, doi:10.1007/978-3-319-54226-3_5.

[10] Ibid., 77.

ary sources in print and online to address those tasks ("looking stuff up"), and iterating toward solutions, refactoring and adding functionality at each pass ("incremental development and iteration").[11]

In our own teaching of the digital humanities, we have erred in both directions, trying either to cram too much programming instruction into a single digital humanities course or to tailor computational concepts too narrowly to the tasks at hand, leaving the students with conceptual gaps.

In spring 2014, Anderson and David A. Michelson, Associate Professor of the History of Christianity at the Vanderbilt Divinity School, co-taught a digital humanities course titled *Topics in Digital Humanities: Introduction to Digital Text Editing and Analysis*.[12] The course provided a general introduction to digital humanities with a focus on the Textual Encoding Initiative (TEI) but also coverage of subjects such as natural language processing in R and geospatial analysis. The class, with seven students enrolled (primarily M.Div. and Th.M. students), met weekly as a seminar for two hours. The programming backgrounds of students in the course varied widely. In most cases, they had no prior experience with programming at all, but a few had extensive experience.

The seminar format turned out to be the most challenging aspect of the course for the teaching of programming. While the seminar format worked well for the theoretical discussions (led by Michelson and Anderson) and adequately for the introduction of methodologies (such as how to employ TEI XML, led by Michelson), Anderson found these weekly sessions were not sufficient to cover programming techniques. While the instructors assigned technical readings in advance, students found it frustrating to read them as the concepts and presentation style were unfamiliar. As a result, Anderson and Michelson spent more time lecturing about these concepts during class than they had intended in order to cover what students had failed to grasp from the readings. This left little opportunity for students to program together during class, increasing the likelihood that they would run into issues when writing code for their projects during the week. To their credit, students managed to submit uniformly excellent final projects. But, looking back on the syllabus, Anderson considers that he tried to introduce too much programming in too short a span. As Mark Guzdial has cautioned, teaching programming in a contextualized course requires that instructors cover less material than they would in a non-contextual-

---

11 Ibid., 78f.
12 For the course website, including the syllabus, see: http://paralipomena.com/. Anecdotally, Anderson and Michelson believe that this was the first course explicitly on the topic of digital humanities offered by an accredited institution of the Association of Theological Schools; as such, the course was expressly experimental.

ized introduction to computer science.¹³ Certainly, it was too ambitious to try to cover XML, TEI, XPath, XQuery, and XML databases along with the R programming language and GIS libraries during a weekly seminar. While the goal was to provide students with a top to bottom perspective on the technology stack of multimodal digital editions, they probably should have focused solely on the XQuery/XPath/XML technologies; as Birnbaum and Langmead indicate, there was no need to teach the fundamentals of computer science, from data types to functions to recursion, to serve the purpose of enabling students to create their own digital editions of religious studies texts. In the next iteration of the course, Michelson and Michelle Taylor, then a postdoc at Vanderbilt University and now Continuing Instructor of English at the University of South Florida, successfully streamlined the course to focus primarily on TEI and the making of digital editions, limiting their coverage of XPath, XQuery, and XML databases to a few case studies rather than providing a fundamental introduction to these tools.

A subsequent digital humanities course Anderson co-taught took a different tack. In fall 2014, he began an informal teaching collaboration with Joy Calico on a one-credit course for undergraduates that explored the history of Berlin in the twentieth century through a series of contemporary maps. By spring 2018, the course had turned into a graduate seminar in the Department of German, Russian and East European Studies, meeting twice weekly. The title of the course, "The Digital Flâneur: Mapping Twentieth-Century Berlin," indicates their approach to teaching technology.[14] Rather than aim to teach students any single programming language systematically, they explored a range of technologies. The first part of the semester examined geospatial information systems, including GeoJSON, online georeferencing tools, and spatially-aware databases. During the second half of the semester, they paraded more quickly from tool to tool, introducing everything from CityGML, Neo4j, the R programming language, to Wikidata. At each stop, Anderson and Calico demonstrated how the particular construct or tool shed new light on the understanding of the city of Berlin.

Intrinsic to digital flânerie is that the instructors never pause long at any single technology. To cover this amount of ground, the class had to keep moving forward. Consequently, students dedicated significant effort outside of class delving into technologies on their own to create their final projects. From a pedagogical perspective, this experience of teaching yourself replicates the learning process of professional digital humanists, preparing graduate students to be-

---

13 Guzdial, "Does Contextualized Computing Education Help?" 5.
14 Clifford B. Anderson and Joy H. Calico, "The Digital Flâneur: Mapping Twentieth-Century Berlin," in *Quick Hits for Teaching with Digital Humanities: Successful Strategies from Award-Winning Teachers*, ed. Christopher J. Young et al. (Bloomington: Indiana University Press, 2020).

come self-reliant when learning new tools and techniques. That said, the instructors had to assist students with their projects in several cases when the technologies could not be assimilated so quickly. For instance, Anderson wrote custom SPARQL queries to retrieve geospatial data from Wikidata and XQuery to transform that data into GeoJSON. Like any tourist operation, digital flânerie works best when students explore the territory in the company of seasoned guides. But how much of such a whirlwind tour remains in students' minds after the semester ends? A course of this sort depends on students' interest in returning to their favorite landmarks, tarrying over overlooked details while also exploring the intersecting boulevards and byways.

3 Teaching the BJC

The proposal for a Beauty and Joy of Computing course arose from discussions about computational thinking with an interdisciplinary group of faculty and staff, including Anderson and Narasimham. In the context of those discussions, Akos Ledeczi (Professor of Computer Engineering and Director of Graduate Studies in Computer Science), Doug Schmidt (Cornelius Vanderbilt Professor of Engineering, Professor of Computer Science, and Professor of Computer Engineering), and Julie Johnson (Professor of the Practice of Computer Science and Director of Undergraduate Studies in Computer Science) invited Anderson to develop a version of the BJC for the School of Engineering. Anderson created the initial version of the course in Fall 2018 and, with lots of help from fellow faculty members, Ledeczi, Brian Broll (research scientist at the Institute for Software Integrated Systems at Vanderbilt University), and Corey Brady (Assistant Professor of Mathematics Education, Department of Teaching and Learning, Peabody School of Education), taught its first three iterations. Narasimham taught the final version of the course in spring 2019. As noted above, Anderson and Narasimham both come from disciplines other than computer science.

The computer science faculty approved the course in spring 2018. The course description read: "Fundamental concepts of computing including abstraction, algorithms, design, and distributed computation. Hands-on curriculum focusing on translating ideas into working computer programs and developing a mastery of practical computational literacy." In practical terms, we planned to address these topics in seven two-week units, promising to teach everything from "control constructs, variables and functions" to "recursion, efficiency, and the limits of computability" with a good measure of networking and distributed computing as well. As we designed the course, we also tried to balance examples from mathematics, science, and the humanities. There is distinct beauty to each of these domains. How to bring it more to the fore in our teaching? Once again, we sought to exemplify a design principle of the BJC: "To help them feel 'CS-smart,' students need to see their code not just as a means to an end with an effect they like but as 'poetry,' code with structure, elegance and power."[15] Our intention was to teach computer science as a way to uncover the inherent beauty of students' home disciplines.

3.1 Goals

We aimed to keep the goals of our offering of the BJC consonant with its original intentions. First, we wanted to provide a rigorous but accessible introduction to computer science to students who felt unprepared for the sequence of programming courses (taught with Java) for majors and minors in computer science. As Dan Garcia stated in a 2012 keynote address, "The purpose of this course is to attract nontraditional computing students (especially women and minorities, but also English majors) to the breadth and depth of ideas in modern computer science."[16] The authors of a recent paper on the design principles behind the BJC underscored this point: "In BJC, our absolute top-level goal is broadened participation in computer science."[17] As with other colleges and universities, we sensed a gap at Vanderbilt in our course offerings for students who wanted to explore the relevance of computer science to their disciplinary interests without committing to learning Java over the course of one or two semesters. We wanted to broaden access to computer science, encouraging students who lacked prior exposure to computer science in high school to consider a minor or double major. But we also sought to convey the fundamentals of computer science to students in the humanities and social sciences who might not have the mathematical prerequisites for a minor or major.

Our course unabashedly taught computational thinking through the discipline of writing, analyzing, and refactoring computer programs. In addition to utility and efficiency, we devoted attention to matters of elegance and style as we examined blocks of code. We stressed functional programming concepts in our teaching because of their inherent elegance without dwelling on the theoretical differences between functional and procedural programming. For instance,

---

15 Paul Goldenberg et al., "Design Principles Behind Beauty and Joy of Computing," in *Proceedings of the 51st ACM Technical Symposium on Computer Science Education*, 2020, 223.
16 Daniel D. Garcia, "The Beauty and Joy of Computing (BJC), AP CS Principles, and the CS 10k Effort," *Journal of Computing Sciences in Colleges* 27, no. 5 (2012): 126–27.
17 Goldenberg et al., "Design Principles Behind Beauty and Joy of Computing," 221.

after teaching students procedural programming concepts such as for and while loops, we showed them how to simplify their programs with functional constructs such as map, filter ("keep"), and reduce ("combine with"). This underlying emphasis on the simplicity and parsimony of functional programming reflects the roots of the BJC curriculum in Scheme. "Berkeley's approach to introductory computer science has been profoundly shaped by the seminal text *Structure and Interpretation of Computer Programs*...," explained Brian Harvey and Jens Mönig in 2010. "In our new course, we wanted to preserve the big ideas we gleaned from their curriculum, including recursion and higher order procedures as organizing tools for flow of control."[18] As we customized the BJC to our context, we aspired to keep that pedagogical heritage intact.

In the first week, we asked students to watch Dan Garcia's presentation of the BJC in a TEDxBerkeley talk from March 2015.[19] During the talk, Garcia uses the program "Vee" to illustrate the surprising elegance of Snap! For those who have not seen "Vee" in action, the program creates a tree with an arbitrary number of leaves and branches. As Harvey and Mönig explain, Vee incorporates sophisticated ideas such as "arbitrarily deep recursion" and treating functions as first-class data while also rendering these concepts more accessible by "focusing students' attention on the recursive case rather than the base case" through the use of randomness.[20] After the midpoint of the semester, students had learned enough to code Vee themselves. In similar fashion, students learned how to create loops during the second week of class and, by the end of the semester, they had mastered enough concepts to create their own looping control structures using higher order functions.

A challenge we faced when adapting the BJC to Vanderbilt was keeping its broad scope while accommodating our course schedule. As Brian Harvey relates, "Berkeley has a 14-week semester, and our course 'The Beauty and Joy of Computing' (BJC) meets seven hours per week: two lecture hours, four lab hours, and one discussion hour."[21] By contrast, our course meet twice a week for seventy-five minutes with no labs or precepts. We divided our classes into two parts, lecturing and leading discussion for the first twenty minutes and then conducting programming exercises during the second two thirds of the class sessions. In stu-

---

18 Brian Harvey and Jens Mönig, "Bringing 'No Ceiling' to Scratch: Can One Language Serve Kids and Computer Scientists?" *Proceedings of Constructionism*, 2010, 3.
19 Daniel D. Garcia, "The Beauty & Joy of Computing," TEDxBerkeley (YouTube, March 25, 2015), https://www.youtube.com/watch?v=ozRovyDwKEM.
20 Harvey and Mönig, "Bringing 'No Ceiling' to Scratch," 4.
21 Brian Harvey, "The Beauty and Joy of Computing: Computer Science for Everyone," *Proceedings of Constructionism*, 2012, 33–39.

dent feedback, we regularly heard that we should devote more time to programming during the course. As with Anderson's prior experience teaching programming in digital humanities contexts, providing the right balance between programming instruction and disciplinary contextualization proved elusive.

3.2 NetsBlox

The Beauty and Joy of Computing course at Berkeley and elsewhere uses the Snap! programming language as its language of instruction.[22] Snap! is a block-based programming language rather than a text-based language. That is, programming in Snap! involves the manipulation of color-coded blocks that snap together to form units of computation. LEGO, the classic children's construction toy, provided the metaphorical inspiration. The most prominent block-based programming language, Scratch, drew inspiration from LEGO bricks when creating its visual syntax. As Mitch Resnick, the Lego Papert Professor of Learning Research and Director of the Lifelong Kindergarten group at MIT, remarks, "In many ways, Scratch is the digital equivalent of the LEGO construction kit."[23]

A significant departure from the standard BJC was our use of NetsBlox rather than Snap! as our programming environment.[24] NetsBlox is a visual programming language which builds on Snap! but which extends its functionality to create a more social experience. Ledeczi leads the development of NetsBlox along with Broll and several graduate students at the School of Engineering.

NetsBlox adds three major features to Snap! to enable communication across networks. First, NetsBlox provides a new primitive for message passing. As Broll, et al., explains, "Messages are very similar to Events already present in Snap! Basically, a Message is an Event that contains data payload."[25] NetsBlox enables message passing between sprites in a project but also across projects, using a unique "public role" identifier that functions something like an email address. Second, NetsBlox adds call and run blocks for making remote procedure calls (RPCs). The blocks encapsulate the APIs of web services, permitting students to connect with remote data sources in their programs. Third, NetsBlox adds the concept of a "room" with "roles" to projects. A "room" provides a way to con-

---

[22] Harvey and Mönig, "Bringing 'No Ceiling' to Scratch."
[23] Mitchel Resnick, *Lifelong Kindergarten: Cultivating Creativity Through Projects, Passion, Peers, and Play* (Cambridge: The MIT Press, 2017), 46.
[24] See https://netsblox.org/.
[25] Brian Broll et al., *NetsBlox: A Visual Language and Web-Based Environment for Teaching Distributed Programming*, 2016. https://netsblox.org/NetsBloxWhitePaper.pdf.

figure a network for a project, allowing users to work on sub-projects in parallel and to connect them (via message passing) using diverse network topologies, allowing for applications like client-server applications.

We drew on these features throughout the course, introducing remote procedure calls during the fourth week while teaching about lists; handling data in the form of lists is the prerequisite for using most RPCs. Right after the midterm, students started exploring message passing, built collaborative whiteboards, and then moved on to a client/server chat application.[26] Our favorite exercise in the class was illustrating person-in-the-middle attacks by asking students to encrypt the messages that they passed through the server (using a substitution cypher) and then having our server break the encryption and subtly alter the message.[27]

3.3 Assessments

Our version of the course had four major assignments. The first was a set of five problems of increasing difficulty. The second was a midterm examination, meant to cover the fundamental programming concepts we taught during the course, from assigning variables to processing lists with higher-order functions. The third was a short paper focusing on a social, historical, or political topic related to computing. We also asked students to develop and present a creative project of their own devising by the end of the semester.

Starting during the second week, we assigned a so-called Parson's Problem every week. For any who are not acquainted with the concept, Dale Parsons and Patricia Haden introduced the idea of creating programming "puzzles" for students to solve rather than asking them to write programs from whole cloth.[28] Parson's Problems seek to make assignments more engaging for students while also limiting the range of possibilities (and errors). An apt comparison would be to chess problems, which set up pieces on the chess board to help learners to rec-

---

[26] Brian Broll et al., "A Visual Programming Environment for Learning Distributed Programming," in *Proceedings of the 2017 ACM SIGCSE Technical Symposium on Computer Science Education*, SIGCSE '17 (Seattle, Washington, USA: Association for Computing Machinery, 2017), 86, doi:10.1145/3017680.3017741.
[27] Broll et al., *NetsBlox*, 6.
[28] Dale Parsons and Patricia Haden, "Parson's Programming Puzzles: A Fun and Effective Learning Tool for First Programming Courses," in *Proceedings of the 8th Australasian Conference on Computing* Education, vol. 52, 2006, 157–63.

ognize and solve certain kinds of tactical problems. We adapted some of the BJC exercises into Parson's Problems while introducing a couple of our own devising.

3.4 Readings

We also departed from the standard BJC approach with our assigned readings. The primary textbook in the BJC is Ken Ledeen, Harry R. Lewis, and Hal Abelson's *Blown to Bits: Your Life, Liberty, and Happiness After the Digital Explosion*.[29] The chapters provide coverage of legal and social topics ranging from copyright law to cryptography. As Brian Harvey noted in 2012, *Blown to Bits* "presents some of the social issues of the Internet era in a style that manages to be both accessible to lay readers and deeply informed by specific technical issues."[30] *Blown to Bits* has aged well for a technical book. Its coverage of §230 of the Communication Decency Act of 1996 remains stubbornly relevant as we continue to debate the merits of its 'safe harbor' provisions for free speech in the age of Facebook and Twitter. Still, the undergraduates taking our course were in primary school when the book first came out, making its discussions dated from their perspective. And the text lacks coverage of topics like algorithmic bias and filter bubbles, which have become major topics of conversation today. A second edition (adding Wendy Seltzer as a co-author) was published in 2021, but not in time for us to use in our course.

We picked up the slack with two other books. The first was Martin Erwig's delightful *Once Upon an Algorithm: How Stories Explain Computing*.[31] As faculty with Ph.D.s in disciplines other than computer science, we wanted to strengthen our presentation of computer science concepts with a strong introductory textbook. While evaluating potential candidates, we ran smack into the problem that most teach computer science via some programming language or another. Eckart Modrow's *Computer Science with Snap!* is unique in its teaching computer science with reference to Snap! but was a bit too advanced for our students– reading the book proved challenging to us![32] Erwig approaches computer science

---

29 Hal Abelson, Ken Ledeen, and Harry Lewis, *Blown to Bits: Your Life, Liberty, and Happiness After the Digital Explosion*, 1st edition (Upper Saddle River, NJ: Addison-Wesley Professional, 2008).
30 Harvey, "The Beauty and Joy of Computing," 1.
31 Martin Erwig, *Once Upon an Algorithm: How Stories Explain Computing* (Cambridge: The MIT Press, 2017).
32 See Eckart Modrow, *Computer Science with Snap!* (Göttingen: Emu-online.de, 2018). See http://ddi-mod.uni-goettingen.de/ComputerScienceWithSnap.pdf.

conceptually, discussing difficult topics like types, recursion, and the limits of computing by reference to books and films like Sherlock Holmes, the "Back to the Future" series, the Indiana Jones movies, and the Harry Potter stories.

Our second assigned reading was Claire Evans's *Broad Band: The Untold Story of the Women Who Made the Internet*.[33] In each chapter of *Broad Band*, Evans presents a vignette or two about women who made significant contributions to computer science. Given her emphasis on the development of networking and communication protocols, Evans's book provided support for our discussions of distributed computing. But her vignettes also helped us to broaden students' perceptions of innovators in computer science, highlighting key women in computing history like Ada Lovelace and Grace Hopper as well as contemporary scientists like Wendy Hall.

We also assigned primary source readings like Alan Turing's "Computing Machinery and Intelligence"[34] during our treatment of Artificial Intelligence. Turing's paper introduces the "imitation game" as a way of evaluating whether a machine had learned to think. Turing also discusses nine potential objections to the notion of thinking machines, which we asked students to consider and evaluate. At the same time, we noted that Turing also introduced problematic opinions, for example, about race relations and Islamic beliefs to his argument. To give students a contemporary perspective on the topic, we paired the reading from Turing with a video by Stephanie Dinkins, new media artist and associate professor in the Department of Art at Stony Brook University. In her video, Dinkins interacts with Bina48, a humanoid robot, on topics ranging from racism to robotic rights.[35]

Our emphasis on course readings perhaps inadvertently gave away our disciplinary origins. As Amy J. Ko, professor at the iSchool at the University of Washington, wrote on Medium: "As a computer science major, I regularly received explicit signals from CS faculty that not only were books irrelevant, but that they were to be explicitly devalued."[36] As a librarian with a background in the humanities and as a social scientist, books are our stock-in-trade. The Beauty and Joy of Computing curriculum encourages reading, discussing, and

---

33 Claire L. Evans, *Broad Band: The Untold Story of the Women Who Made the Internet* (New York: Portfolio, 2018).
34 A. M. Turing, "Computing Machinery and Intelligence," *Mind* LIX, no. 236 (October 1950): 433–60, doi:10.1093/mind/LIX.236.433.
35 See https://www.stephaniedinkins.com/conversations-with-bina48.html.
36 Amy J. Ko, "Computer Science Taught Me That Books Weren't Important. It Was Wrong." *Medium*, July 2020. See https://medium.com/bits-and-behavior/computer-science-taught-me-that-books-werent-important-it-was-wrong-63ead2fdad7a.

writing about social issues related to computing, but the "Get Ready to Read" flairs we saw from students on Rate My Professor probably meant the quantity of assigned readings surprised them.

3.5 Final Projects

We dedicated the second half of the semester to the final project. After the midterm, we lectured on topics ranging from recursion to computational complexity, but we did not test the students on those subjects, wishing to avoid anxiety about these traditionally difficult concepts. Students devoted themselves instead to final projects that they presented to one another during the final week of the semester. Our goal with the final paper and project was to encourage students to contextualize what they had learned about computing to their domains of interest.

The range of projects varied widely from simple games (like Slither.IO clones) to literary and scientific programs. A few students worked on computational poetry generators. An ambitious student implemented and visualized a single linkage clustering algorithm that she had learned in her biology course. A significant number of projects drew on data from NetsBlox RPCs. If students wished to work in pairs, we required them to make use of NetsBlox message passing features. Students who took this team option developed two-player soccer games and also a peer-to-peer Venmo-like application.

We also asked students to argue critically for an ethical or social stance related to computing. Over the four semesters we taught the class, several students selected topics that stood on the boundary between religion and computer science. Students, for instance, considered that Turing had dismissed the soul as a dividing line between human beings and machines too quickly.[37] This is perhaps not too surprising as limit concepts in computer science, from artificial intelligence to the possibility of super-intelligence, touch on theological issues. When Anderson was invited as a guest lecturer for another course, "The Ethics of Artificial Intelligence," students had expressed similar curiosity about what makes human beings distinctive and whether artificial intelligence would become a companion, savior, or devil to humanity.[38] In her teaching of ethics to students of computer science, Narasimham emphasizes the human factor in computing errors and considers situations from multiple humanistic perspectives

---

[37] Turing, "Computing Machinery and Intelligence," 443f.
[38] See https://my.vanderbilt.edu/aiethics/.

(as well as legal precedents, where applicable) when deciding on their ethicality, calling for more nuanced reasoning rather than just reliance on rigid algorithmic principles. Students in her class also debate freedom of speech issues with respect to the use of technology and the internet to express religious thoughts that may be contentious among certain groups but acceptable to others.

3.6 Reception

The course never took off in the way that we hoped at Vanderbilt. We offered the class over four consecutive semesters and enrollment averaged fewer than twenty students per offering. While the enrollment statistics would have been sufficient for most humanities courses to make, they fell short of expectations at the School of Engineering. Given the surging interest in computer science, any course that does not approach its enrollment cap cannot be sustained.

The most significant mismatch was the institutional setting. The School of Engineering offered the course, but the majority of students came from other schools at Vanderbilt, primarily the College of Arts and Science but also Peabody College of Education and the Blair School of Music. From our initial survey of students' goals for the course, these students recognized the significance of computer science for their future careers, but most had not had the opportunity to study computer science at the high school level. The sequence of courses for majors and minors in computer science would represent too great a commitment and possibly prove overwhelming. But the Beauty and Joy of Computing proved too elementary for most students enrolled at the School of Engineering. (The exception were a few advanced CS students who said they took this course to get a perspective on programming in non-CS fields.) The problem was that our course did not fulfill the graduation requirements required for students at the College of Arts and Science, which meant they took it as a pure elective. For better or worse, the students who took our course wanted to be there as they had no extrinsic reason for enrolling beyond interest in computing (and generic course credit). We speculate that the course would have received more registrations if it had been listed in a college other than the School of Engineering. This raises the question, what would a more contextualized version of the BJC, say for the Divinity School, look like?

4 Computational Thinking and Learning

In the past year, the Computational Thinking and Learning Initiative (CTLI) at Vanderbilt University has explored questions about the contextualization of computer science instruction.[39] The CTLI is an institutionally-supported interdisciplinary group of faculty and staff that seeks to expand computer science across the curriculum. The group gathers together researchers from disciplines such as computer science, education, information science, and the humanities to strategize about scaling computational thinking to all students at Vanderbilt (and beyond).

The members of the CTLI are broadly concerned with the question of teaching programming in disciplines other than computer science. As mentioned at the outset of this paper, programming is already being taught in many non-CS contexts at Vanderbilt and other colleges and universities, albeit often not in systematic ways. Michelson and Anderson trained students in the rudiments of the XQuery programming language. In the "Digital Flâneur" course, Calico and Anderson instructed students about data structures when showing them how to encode geospatial data in JSON and also gave them a practical introduction to remote procedure calls by walking through how to send that encoded JSON data using REST calls to CouchDB. Narasimham led an interdisciplinary working group on data visualization for several years while a staff member of the Vanderbilt Institute for Digital Learning. A colleague in Cinema and Media Arts is teaching Processing to students and a faculty member in the Department of French and Italian is training undergraduates in C# to create historical games with the Unity game engine. During the past year, faculty in the digital humanities have begun to put together a curricular sequence to link disparate courses. What can be learned from the way that programming is being taught in these contexts? This question harkens back to a remark by Eric Roberts during SIGCSE discussions about the Beauty and Joy of Computing from 2009: "If we want to produce software artists, it might be useful to experiment with alternative educational strategies similar to those used to prepare artists, writers, and musicians."[40]

The CTLI sponsors several working groups that bring together faculty, staff, and students to connect computer science education with topics from specific

---

[39] See https://alo.ees.vanderbilt.edu/ctli/.
[40] Daniel D. Garcia et al., "Rediscovering the Passion, Beauty, Joy, and Awe: Making Computing Fun Again, Continued," in *Proceedings of the 40th Acm Technical Symposium on Computer Science Education*, 2009, 65–66.

domains. These working groups are exploring how students can learn to program in NetsBlox with reference to the problem of climate change, on the one hand, and textual analysis, on the other. In a related ongoing study, Narasimham is collaborating with Gautam Biswas (Professor of Engineering and Professor of Computer Science, Computer Engineering, and Engineering Management, as well as member of the CTLI) and researchers from the department of computer science to explore how high school students may use NetsBlox to learn both computing and physics concepts.

Anderson and Mark Schoenfield, Professor of English in the College of Arts and Science at Vanderbilt, coordinate the "Modalities of Textual Analysis" working group with Brady and Broll. The group is co-sponsored by the CTLI and the Vanderbilt University Libraries. The libraries support the activities of the working group through its endowed Buchanan Fellowship program, which provides fellowships for undergraduates to work together with librarians and faculty on topics of strategic value to the libraries.[41] During the spring and fall semesters of 2019, fellows explored the affordances of NetsBlox for conducting textual analysis of ProQuest's British Periodicals database. The database consists of the full text of nearly five hundred British periodicals and several million articles, dating from the seventeenth to the twentieth centuries. To make it possible for students to search across these articles for keywords and phrases, the principals put the XML documents into a BaseX database. Broll built an integration into NetsBlox to send and receive requests to BaseX while Anderson built a small library of blocks to encapsulate the XQuery requests. The blocks allow students to look up information from the British Periodicals without having to write any XQuery code, send REST requests, or parse JSON data. Results from British Periodicals come back as a list of lists, which students can pass directly to other functions in their program. By the end of the semester, students were able to carry out the main steps of text analysis, from gathering a dataset, cleaning the data, applying various natural language processing operations, summarizing the results, and producing visualizations–all within NetsBlox.[42]

---

[41] Library Communications, "Buchanan Gift to Endow Vanderbilt Library Fellowship Program," *Library News Online*, January 2018. See https://newsonline.library.vanderbilt.edu/2018/01/buchanan-gift-to-endow-vanderbilt-library-fellowship-program/.

[42] For more information about the pilot, see Brian Broll et al., "A Blocks-Based Introduction to Text Analysis," Snap!Con 2020, July 2020. See https://forum.snap.berkeley.edu/t/short-talk-a-blocks-based-introduction-to-text-analysis/2576.

5 The Telos of Block-Based Programming

There is ongoing debate about the utility of introducing students to programming through block-based environments.[43] How does starting students out in a block-based environment affect their long-term success as programmers?

On the one hand, the visual metaphor of programming by snapping blocks together seems to strike an intuitive chord with students while also encouraging a sense of playful exploration. The sense of playfulness shows the line of descent of these environments from Seymour Papert, whose "constructionism" encouraged children to learn by assimilating examples from a domain and then playing with them.[44] In a talk at Digital Humanities 2019 in Utrecht, Anderson and Lynn Ramey, professor of French at Vanderbilt University and the faculty director of Vanderbilt's Digital Humanities Center, argued that block-based environments, when suitably adjusted, could help digital humanists learn to code more effectively.[45] While preserving the ludic experience of programming with blocks, they suggested creating a version of NetsBlox with RPCs for popular digital humanities services, sprites that represent relevant objects of computation, and a curriculum aimed at humanists.

A drawback to using block-based programming environments is the perception of them as programming cul-de-sacs, if not dead ends. While learning to program in block-based environments may speed the learning process for students by reducing the possibility of making syntax errors and encouraging an exploratory and tinkering style of coding, it seems inevitable that students will eventually need to transition to text-based languages like JavaScript, Python, or XQuery. But can that transition be delayed? The aspiration of making software environments "low threshold" but "high ceiling" is attributed to Papert, inventor of the Logo programming language. As Brad Myers, Scott E. Hudson, and Randy Pausch put the idea, "The 'threshold' is how difficult it is to learn how to use the

---

[43] Zhen Xu et al., "Block-Based Versus Text-Based Programming Environments on Novice Student Learning Outcomes: A Meta-Analysis Study," *Computer Science Education* 29, nos. 2–3 (July 2019): 177–204, doi:10.1080/08993408.2019.1565233; Yue Hu, Cheng-Huan Chen, and Chien-Yuan Su, "Exploring the Effectiveness and Moderators of Block-Based Visual Programming on Student Learning: A Meta-Analysis," *Journal of Educational Computing Research* 58, no. 8 (January 2021): 1467–93, doi:10.1177/0735633120945935.
[44] Seymour A. Papert, *Mindstorms: Children, Computers, and Powerful Ideas*, Revised edition (Basic Books, 2020), 133.
[45] Clifford B. Anderson and Lynn T. Ramey, "Thinking Computationally in the Digital Humanities: Toward Block-Based Programming for Humanists" (Utrecht: DataverseNL, December 2019), doi:10.34894/7QDKAP.

system, and the 'ceiling' is how much can be done using the system."⁴⁶ Proponents and critics alike typically agree that block-based environments are "low threshold." In our classrooms, we have witnessed the delight of non-programmers experimenting with stacks of coding blocks in Snap!, generating shifting graphical effects on the stage. Playing with graphics of a similar sort in C++ or Java would be considered an advanced exercise. But do block-based environments provide sufficiently "high ceilings"? A motivation for creating the Snap! programming language was a concern that Scratch had, in fact, oversimplified the language. The goal of creating Snap! was "to extend the power of Scratch to more advanced computer science ideas, suitable for an undergraduate CS course."⁴⁷ While professors of computer science have used Snap! to demonstrate advanced concepts in computer science,⁴⁸ the attitude persists among students that block-based languages are intended for children or rank beginners. In a computer science course that used Scratch during the first two weeks of an introductory course before switching to Java, the instructors reported that "some students associate Scratch with pre-university education, thus they consider its use childish and 'non-serious.'"⁴⁹ An active area of research in computer science education is when and how best to transition students away from these environments. "Many uses of block-based tools in formal educational contexts presuppose that such tools will help prepare students for later instruction in text-based languages," write David Weintrop and Uri Wilensky. "This transition is often a part of the larger computer science trajectory where block-based introductory courses are intended to prepare students for the transition to professional, text-based languages."⁵⁰ If students eventually need to leave the block-based environment behind as part of their programming journey, they may be forgiven for wondering whether they should have started there in the first place.

---

46 Brad Myers, Scott E. Hudson, and Randy Pausch, "Past, Present, and Future of User Interface Software Tools," *ACM Transactions on Computer-Human Interaction* 7, no. 1 (March 2000): 6, doi:10.1145/344949.344959.
47 B. Harvey and J. Mönig, "Lambda in Blocks Languages: Lessons Learned," in *2015 IEEE Blocks and Beyond Workshop (Blocks and Beyond)*, 2015, 35, doi:10.1109/BLOCKS.2015.7368997.
48 Eckart Modrow, *Computer Science with Snap!*
49 José Alfredo Martínez-Valdés, J. Ángel Velázquez-Iturbide, and Raquel Hijón-Neira, "A (Relatively) Unsatisfactory Experience of Use of Scratch in CS1," in *Proceedings of the 5th International Conference on Technological Ecosystems for Enhancing Multiculturality*, TEEM 2017 (New York, NY, USA: Association for Computing Machinery, 2017), 1–7, doi:10.1145/3144826.3145356.
50 David Weintrop and Uri Wilensky, "Transitioning from Introductory Block-Based and Text-Based Environments to Professional Programming Languages in High School Computer Science Classrooms," *Computers & Education* 142 (December 2019): 2, doi:10.1016/j.compedu.2019.103646, internal references omitted.

In a Viewpoint piece in *Communications of the ACM,* David Weintrop questions whether students must all eventually transition away from block-based programming: "If it is possible to do significant, non-trivial tasks in block-based environments, should we still expect all learners, even those not likely to pursue a degree in computer science, to learn text-based programming?"[51] In Anderson's use of NetsBlox in textual analysis with undergraduate students, he has observed a different phenomenon. The students who take part in the working group come with different levels of exposure to computer science. Some students arrive with a major or minor in computer science while others have never had any formal or informal coding experience. To level the playing field, we start out the entire group in NetsBlox. The functional programming structures that we tend to favor in our programming exercises are sufficiently new to students with previous coding experience that everybody learns together during the first few weeks. As the semester progresses, we encourage students to complement NetsBlox with other programming languages and frameworks. Experienced students may, for instance, export a list from NetsBlox as a CSV file to a natural language processing library in Python or a visualization tool to carry out a procedure not yet achievable within NetsBlox. Students can also re-import that data to NetsBlox, converting CSV or JSON into a list of lists. By fostering a porous computational environment that makes data readily transferable, the question of when and how best to transition to a text-based environment seems less pertinent. Rather, students come to appreciate text-based programming tools as well as other visual development environments alongside NetsBlox. In the end, our goal is not to promote either modality, but to encourage a "human-centered" design approach to teaching computation to humanists where one size does not fit all.[52]

In "Design Principles for Tools to Support Creative Thinking," Mitchel Resnick et al. added the concept of "wide walls" to Papert's "low threshold" and "high ceiling."[53] What they mean by "wide walls" is that a creative learning environment should serve many purposes and not be tailored toward predeter-

---

51 David Weintrop, "Block-Based Programming in Computer Science Education," *Communications of the ACM* 62, no. 8 (July 2019): 25, doi:10.1145/3341221.
52 Clifford B. Anderson et al., "Human-Centered Computing for Humanists: Case Studies from the Computational Thinking and Learning Initiative at Vanderbilt University," Short Paper, DH2020, July 2020 (Not held due to COVID-19). See https://dh2020.adho.org/wp-content/uploads/2020/07/681_HumanCenteredComputingforHumanistsCaseStudiesfromtheComputationalThinkingandLearningInitiativeatVanderbiltUniversity.html.
53 Mitchel Resnick et al., "Design Principles for Tools to Support Creative Thinking," January 2005, 3, doi:10.1184/R1/6621917.v1.

mined uses. "The design challenge is to be specific enough so that users can quickly understand how to use the features (low threshold)," they write, "but general enough so that users can continue to find new ways to use them (wide walls)."[54] The metaphor of "wide walls" provides a different frame for students' use of technologies to supplement NetsBlox. Given that developers can easily incorporate new remote procedure calls (RPCs) to NetsBlox, encouraging students to explore related technologies also helps to identify potential integrations.

For instance, Broll added an integration for ParallelDots, a commercial natural language processing service, to NetsBlox so that students could, for instance, analyze the sentiment of strings from texts.[55] After experimenting with using the service to discern the sentiment of eighteenth and nineteenth century texts, students also came to appreciate the limitations of applying a NLP model evidently trained on contemporary internet discourse (like YouTube comments and restaurant reviews) to periodical literature from a different time period. Later during the semester, Broll incorporated Stanford's CoreNLP[56] as another RPC for natural language processing. CoreNLP provides a wide variety of annotators, including a sentiment analysis tool. This integration permitted students to compare the results of natural language toolkits, sharpening their critical sense of their respective uses and limitations.

Anderson is also experimenting with a remote procedure call to link NetsBlox with Wikidata for easy access to cultural heritage data.[57] As mentioned above, Anderson and Calico introduced graduate students to Wikidata in their "Digital Flâneur" seminar. Students took quickly to the user interface for data entry, but experienced greater difficulty with the query interface and also had trouble converting data from Wikidata into other formats. To address these issues, Anderson and Broll have collaborated on a remote procedure call that allows NetsBlox users to send parameterized SPARQL queries to the Wikidata Query Service and to receive data back in the form of a NetsBlox list of lists.[58] If Anderson and Calico were to teach the course again, they would be able to

---

54 Ibid., 4.
55 Broll et al., "A Blocks-Based Introduction to Text Analysis."
56 Christopher Manning et al., "The Stanford CoreNLP Natural Language Processing Toolkit," in *Proceedings of 52nd Annual Meeting of the Association for Computational Linguistics: System Demonstrations* (Baltimore: Association for Computational Linguistics, 2014), 55–60, doi:10.3115/v1/P14–5010.
57 Clifford B. Anderson, "Teaching with Wikidata: A Case Study," *Wikiconference North America 2018* (Columbus, 2018).
58 Ibid.

use NetsBlox as an environment for much of their flânerie, permitting students to spend more time analyzing the different ways of representing urban environments digitally while spending less time on software engineering concepts like source control systems and data structures like JSON and XML.

The customization of NetsBlox into a platform for playfully exploring with computational techniques in the digital humanities while achieving digital humanities *tasks* will require careful balancing. From the perspective of professional tools, NetsBlox may seem too barebones. A Python, Node, or R library exists for every conceivable computational task. But Snap! and NetsBlox come only with a few libraries of routines. A reason for this parsimony is the desire to maintain simplicity. An additional reason is that Snap! and NetsBlox seek to encourage students to explore *how* to build these libraries for themselves. For this reason, they do not come prepackaged with searching and sorting routines, but students can learn to instantiate their own algorithms for this purpose. As Mary Angelec Cooksey remarks about her use of Raspberry Pis in the classroom, "In a course like the Philosophy of Computing, teachers want students to see what is going on with computing at its most basic level."[59] As NetsBlox becomes capable of solving more and more *tasks* in the digital humanities, we must also be careful to maintain this kind of pedagogical minimalism.

The ability of educational environments like Processing[60] successfully to span the gap between learning platform and professional programming tool in new media encourages us about the potential of NetsBlox to serve similar ends in the humanities. As the number of RPCs for NetsBlox increases, students of religious studies can already carry out a wide range of context relevant tasks: mapping the locations of houses of worship in a particular region, identifying people or events mentioned in sermons, and searching for trending religious topics on Twitter, among much else. As students and scholars of religious studies and theology increasingly engage with the digital humanities, we hope that these activities can be integrated into a version of the Beauty and Joy of Computing that faculty may use to teach computation in a context-relevant way in seminary and divinity school classrooms.

---

59 Mary Angelec Cooksey, "Teaching the Philosophy of Computing Using the Raspberry Pi," in *Quick Hits for Teaching with Digital Humanities: Successful Strategies from Award-Winning Teachers*, ed. Christopher J. Young et al., Illustrated edition (Bloomington, Indiana, USA: Indiana University Press, 2020), 56.
60 Casey Reas and Ben Fry, "Processing: Programming for the Media Arts," *AI & SOCIETY* 20, no. 4 (September 2006): 526–38, doi:10.1007/s00146-006-0050-9.

IV Collaboration and Beyond

Experimental Humanities Lab at the Iliff School of Theology
Library as Interface for Digital Humanities

1 Introduction

Over the last decade, there have been many challenging and useful explorations of the potential relationships between libraries and emerging digital humanities scholarship (DH). Early on, this literature focused on the role libraries could play in digitizing research materials and building digital collections. Libraries have expanded this role to also host and maintain DH projects; in fact, Kretzschmar and Potter argue that academic libraries are the "only realistic option" for the sustainability of DH projects.[1] Much of the literature on libraries and DH has highlighted the ways in which libraries have supported researchers in various DH projects. Of course, supporting research is not new to libraries. What is unique about DH projects is that librarians are moving from supportive roles to collaborative partners.[2] There is no shortage of case studies documenting such collaboration.[3] The literature also includes resources for those librarians who may not know how to get involved or what skills they may need. Hartsell-Gundy et al. have edited a volume containing many essays which provide instruction on libraries and DH, especially for subject specialists.[4] In fall 2017, the journal *College and Undergraduate Libraries* devoted an entire issue to the sub-

---

[1] William A. Kretzschmar and William Gray Potter, "Library Collaboration with Large Digital Humanities Projects," *Literary & Linguistic Computing* 25, no. 4 (December 2010): 439–45, https://doi.org/10.1093/llc/fqq022.
[2] Jane Harvell and Joanna Ball, "Why We Need to Find Time for Digital Humanities: Presenting a New Partnership Model at the University of Sussex," *Insights: The UKSG Journal* 30, no. 3 (November 2017): 38–43, https://doi.org/10.1629/uksg.377.
[3] For a few select recent examples see Janet Bunde and Deena Engel, "Computing in the Humanities: An Interdisciplinary Partnership in Undergraduate Education," *Journal of Archival Organization* 8, no. 2 (April 2010): 149–59, https://doi.org/10.1080/15332748.2010.519993; A. Miller, "DS/DH Start-Ups: A Library Model for Advancing Scholarship through Collaboration," *Journal of Web Librarianship* 10, no. 2 (April 2016): 83–100, https://doi.org/10.1080/19322909.2016.1149544; Marissa Mourer, "A Subject Librarian's Pedagogical Path in the Digital Humanities," *College & Undergraduate Libraries* 24, no. 2–4 (October 2, 2017): 501–15, https://doi.org/10.1080/10691316.2017.1336506; Janet Hauck, "From Service to Synergy: Embedding Librarians in a Digital Humanities Project," *College & Undergraduate Libraries* 24, no. 2–4 (October 2, 2017): 434–51, https://doi.org/10.1080/10691316.2017.1341357.
[4] Arianne Hartsell-Gundy, Laura Braunstein, and Liorah Golomb, *Digital Humanities in the Library: Challenges and Opportunities for Subject Specialists* (ACRL, 2015), 309.

 OpenAccess. © 2021 Experimental Humanities Lab at the Iliff School of Theology, published by De Gruyter. This work is licensed under the Creative Commons Attribution-NonCommercial-NoDerivatives 4.0 International License. https://doi.org/10.1515/9783110536539-010

ject of DH in academic libraries. This issue addressed topics such as theoretical perspectives, collaboration, project management, the ACRL framework and DH, and embedded library instruction related to DH. Finally, dh + lib, "Where digital humanities and librarianship meet," is an excellent resource for all things DH and librarianship.[5] Our goal in this chapter is to add our own voices to the conversation by discussing the place of theological and religious studies libraries in the current DH environment and to share a little of our own experience in promoting DH in our own context.

From our experience starting an Experimental[6] Humanities Lab in the Taylor Library at the Iliff School of Theology, we would like to add two ideas to advocate for the important role religious and theological libraries can play in driving digital humanities research. First, religious and theological libraries are particularly well suited to foster DH research given the constitutive interdisciplinarity of the study of religion which these kinds of libraries support. Second, conceptualizing libraries as interfaces that afford digital humanities work reinforces the values and material practices shared by libraries and DH.

2 Interdisciplinary Dispositions

Theology and religious studies have always been characterized by bringing together methodologies and theories from several disciplines such as anthropology, history, philosophy, and media studies. Theology, historically, has been interdisciplinary. For example, the model of theological education most often followed in U.S. seminaries and divinity schools follows the plan outlined by Friedrich Schleiermacher in 1811, who defined theology as a "technical" rather than a "pure" science, because theology brings together historians, philoso-

---

5 "Dh+lib," dh+lib, accessed September 13, 2018, https://acrl.ala.org/dh/.
6 Our lab initially developed without the need for a name. We were just a group of people who were interested in learning some natural language processing together on a regular basis. As we started to talk with more people about what we were doing and participating in conferences, it became useful to have a name for our group. While we were considering this branding in early 2015, we bumped into a tweet from Miriam Posner (https://twitter.com/miriamkp/status/570369790436446210) that mentioned Nicholas Bauch's preference for "Experimental Humanities" over "Digital Humanities" and mentioned Maria Sachiko Cecire, the director of the Center for Experimental Humanities at Bard College. Though "experimental" and "lab" are somewhat redundant, we were compelled by the focus on trying new methodologies signaled by "experimental" more than the strict computational focus of the "digital." So, we took Bard's lead and branded our group the Experimental Humanities Lab @ Iliff (https://www.iliff.edu/experimental-humanities/).

phers, sociologists, exegetes of ancient texts, etc., for the common purpose of training religious leaders. Religious Studies, as distinct from theology, is a more recent field. The "classic" texts Ph.D. students are expected to master in a typical theories and methods course in the academic study of religion come largely from philosophy (Hume, Kant, Foucault, et al.), anthropology (Geertz, Bourdieu, Asad, et al.), and sociology (Durkheim, Weber, et al.). Recent dissertation committees in our institutions have included economists, psychologists, musicologists, and law faculty, to name just a few. This disposition toward making connections between different approaches and doing the hard work of negotiating across discourses positions librarians, students, and faculty in religious studies well for participating in the interdisciplinary work of DH.

As Timothy Beal suggested at a talk on the future of the academic study of religion in the twilight of print book culture,

> The academic study of religion has really never been a discipline in any common sense of the term; rather, individually and collectively, we draw on a range of traditional and emerging disciplines, from ethnographic to sociological to narratological to cognitive-scientific. Indeed, religious studies is better conceived not as a *discipline* but as an *interdisciplinary field* whose boundaries are under constant renegotiation. What Jonathan Z. Smith argued with regard to the ways we religionists interpret and represent religion is also true of the ways we interpret and represent the field of academic religious studies itself: we make and remake schematic maps of it, constantly negotiating matters of fit and placement in the process.[7]

Beal highlights the constant process of making connections and reaching across disciplinary boundaries that constitutes the academic study of religion. As we will see in our definitions of digital humanities below, the interdisciplinarity of the study of religion lends itself to participation in digital humanities work.

3 Library as Interface

In light of the proliferation of internet interfaces that reduce users to simple, deterministic consumers, Johanna Drucker asks humanists to get more serious about developing a theory of interface that considers the entanglement of user (she prefers subject) and material platform in the collaborative construction of

---

[7] Timothy Beal, "Faith in Chaos: Interdisciplinary Emergencies and Emergences in Religious Studies." presented at Conversations with Tim Beal, University of Denver, Denver CO, May 11, 2015.

digital spaces.[8] Resisting the overly simplistic window metaphor often used to describe digital interfaces, Drucker suggests that an interface is a zone of encounter that provokes probabilistic production.[9] Rather than simply providing a benign portal to content that a user consumes, an interface is the space constructed by the encounter between a user's activity and the material structures of a screen or a mobile device or an internet browser. If we take reading as an example of use, this zone of encounter, this entanglement of user and material platform, *provokes* a collaborative *production* of meaning as a reader participates in the materiality of a reading technology (roll, codex, e-reader) to create the reading event. This production is *probabilistic* because the reading event is new every time and is fashioned by the ways in which a specific encounter selectively marshals the possibilities provided by the potential combinations of user needs and platform capabilities. In this event of encounter, which constitutes interface, neither user nor technology are reduced to some deterministic entity in service of simple consumption.[10]

Drucker's sophisticated notion of interface seems a fitting metaphor for how libraries function in this emerging digital age. Far from any simple reduction to a repository of information that users come to consume, libraries operate as zones of encounter that provoke probabilistic production. It is this notion of library as interface that makes libraries ideal spaces to empower digital humanities work within an institution. The combination of collaboration, interdisciplinarity, and attention to materiality operative in libraries at institutions focused on theology and religious studies make them ideal laboratories for the exploration of the rich potential of digital humanities.

4 Libraries Embody DH Values

This assertion that libraries are the most fitting spaces for the pursuit of digital humanities in academic institutions begs a more precise definition of digital humanities. There are several operative definitions of digital humanities floating

---

8 Johanna Drucker, "Humanities Approaches to Interface Theory," *Culture Machine* 12, no. 0 (February 18, 2011), https://www.culturemachine.net/index.php/cm/article/view/434.
9 Drucker, 7–9, 18. Her exact phrasing for interface here is "zone of affordances," but given that affordances articulate a possible encounter between environment and user, we have highlighted this notion of encounter in the shift to interface as "zone of encounter."
10 Johanna Drucker, "Entity to Event: From Literal, Mechanistic Materiality to Probabilistic Materiality," *Parallax* 15, no. 4 (November 1, 2009): 7–17, https://doi.org/10.1080/13534640903208834 provides additional helpful exploration of reading as a probabilistic event.

around the current discourse and many of the current working definitions of digital humanities (DH) suggest a strong correlation with values and practices long embodied by libraries. For example, Burdick et al. offer a concise definition of DH that highlights collaboration, interdisciplinarity, and awareness of the importance of medium, suggesting that

> Digital Humanities refers to new modes of scholarship and institutional units for collaborative, transdisciplinary, and computationally engaged research, teaching, and publication. Digital Humanities is less a unified field than an array of convergent practices that explore a universe in which print is no longer the primary medium in which knowledge is produced and disseminated.[11]

Libraries are institutional units that have long embodied these DH values of collaboration, interdisciplinarity, and attention to medium.

5 Collaboration

The Experimental Humanities Lab at Iliff School of Theology is a product of this return to library as collaborative space. In the past four years, Iliff has shifted collection practices and reconfigured physical space to encourage patrons and library staff to use the library as a place for constructive collaborative dialog and design. The reference collection and bound periodicals collection which had occupied the main floor of Iliff's library were carefully weeded or moved to other locations while technology was added (large screens, wireless projection, and webcams) that enabled groups to use the space to explore questions and projects together. From this space emerged our Experimental Humanities Lab at Iliff. On the heels of some graduate students doing research at the intersection of religious studies and digital humanities, a few students, staff and faculty started gathering weekly to learn the basics of natural language processing in Python together using the *Natural Language Toolkit Book* as a starting point.[12] Through additional collaborative endeavors, such as our involvement in a DH project with the Baker Nord Center at Case Western Reserve University and our facilitation of THATCamps at the annual meeting of the American Academy of

---

11 Anne Burdick et al., *Digital_Humanities* (Cambridge, MA: MIT Press, 2012), 122. The authors have also released an open access *Short Guide to Digital_Humanities*, which is an excerpt from this text available at http://jeffreyschnapp.com/wp-content/uploads/2013/01/D_H_ShortGuide.pdf

12 Steven Bird, Ewan Klein, and Loper, "NLTK Book," accessed October 3, 2018, https://www.nltk.org/book/.

Religion and the American Theological Library Association, others have joined our weekly gatherings from other institutions, such as Case Western Reserve University, George Mason University, and the American Theological Library Association. Having collaborators from multiple contexts has helped broaden our learning by exposing us to different problems and different tool sets than those we might focus on at our institution.

As this Experimental Humanities Lab in the library at Iliff has matured, we have noticed another kind of collaboration emerge. We have come to consider machines as collaborators in the reading, writing, and research process. More than simply tools, machine learning models and the algorithms involved in them are teaching us new things, raising interesting questions, and exposing us to different viewpoints. As partners in research, machines add an important voice into the discovery and analysis process that can challenge our assumptions and open avenues toward difference.

Text generation is one example of the kinds of tasks we have explored as a group to develop basic competencies with machine learning and to explore theoretical questions related to machines as partners in the reading and writing process. For example, we trained a neural network on past issues of the *Iliff Review* (64,412 sentences) and then asked three questions of the resulting model: (1) What is Iliff?[13] (2) Who is God? and (3) Who is Jesus? Our goal was to find answers to these questions based upon decades of essays that might generate various answers to these questions. Our neural network came up with the following answers:

Table 1: Neural Network Text Generation Results

WHAT IS ILIFF?	WHO IS GOD?	WHO IS JESUS?
Iliff is the creative destruction.	God is required for question.	Jesus is baptist belonging!
Iliff is feeling for the teaching?	God is magic.	Jesus is recovery.
Iliff is doctrinal meaningless.	God is peculiar creative volume.	Jesus is limiting this one?
Iliff is sage and whites.	God is answered and specialized.	Jesus is doing communion.
Iliff is creative may be village.	God is true for a third autobiography.	Jesus is frequent textual.
Iliff is more painful.	God is simply with others and will be constructive.	
Iliff is subjective too.		

---

13 This question seems apropos in light of the fact that this publication was published by the Iliff School of Theology.

Some of the above answers might seem like they are worded just a little differently from how a human being might word such an answer, but we have to remember that machines are working with a limited vocabulary (the vocabulary we feed them),[14] and they may try to express things that go beyond our natural syntax given their limited vocabulary. Inquiring of a machine in this way may require us to put forth effort in an attempt to understand an entity that has a non-human (machinic) perspective. What might we glean from the above answers? Take, for example, the first answer, "What is Iliff?" The machine first responded "Iliff is the creative destruction." This response may seem nonsensical to some readers, but at the Iliff School of Theology there has been an attempt to deconstruct (or "destroy," in language our model might use) unjust social structures. Similarly, some at Iliff have taken interest in how we might reconstruct (or "create," in language our model might understand) social structures that are more just. When we shared this statement with a few faculty, they were struck by how this statement strikes at the heart of what some faculty at Iliff are attempting to do. This approach might seem like an attempt to consult an Iliff oracle in the way one might consult the Oracle at Delphi,[15] but each of the above statements makes some sense based upon Iliff's historical context as given in the pages of the *Iliff Review*.

6 Interdisciplinarity

Interdisciplinarity is another characteristic of digital humanities highlighted by the definition quoted above. Digital humanities projects 1) demand an interdisciplinary approach, 2) create possibilities for new connections between disciplines, and 3) can leverage the already active interdisciplinary methodologies of religious studies.
1) At the most basic level, DH projects demand interaction between a humanities discipline and expertise from data science, often including programm-

---

14 For this particular project, we further limited the vocabulary by removing rare words in order to expedite the fitting of the model.
15 Ancient oracles were often notoriously ambiguous. For example, Herodotus tells the story of how the Lacedaemonians understood a certain oracle to mean that they would defeat their neighbors the Tegeans, so they brought shackles with them when they went out to meet them (1.66.3). As it turned out, the Lacedaemonians misinterpreted the oracle, and the Lacedaemonian survivors ended up being bound by the very shackles they had brought (1.66.4).

ers.[16] This cooperation means that DH work is always interdisciplinary from the ground up, demanding both humanities scholars and data scientists to learn from one another.

2) Additionally, research projects focused on bringing datasets together to explore phenomena can also create new possibilities for interaction among different disciplines that might typically be unaware of one another. For example, building a neural network to identify and analyze racial bias in religious discourse in contemporary social media rhetoric may require the construction of a dataset and development of computational models using tools and methodologies from religion, sociology, media studies, and mathematics. Each of these disciplines might inform the categories and data types used in the dataset in sometimes sophisticated ways.

3) As we noted above, this interdisciplinary approach to digital humanities may also give religious studies and theological libraries a strategic advantage in providing a platform for digital humanities work. Religious studies, like DH, is often talked about as an interdisciplinary endeavor. Much of the research done in religious studies draws on methodologies and expertise from disciplines such as anthropology, history, sociology, philosophy, and media studies. Libraries and librarians already accustomed to supporting this kind of research that reaches into other disciplines are well positioned to support the inherently interdisciplinary work of DH projects.

7 Materiality of Information

Another strong emphasis we see in the definition of DH we cited above is the importance of the materiality of information, connecting DH to the twilight of print as the dominant medium for the production and dissemination of knowledge.[17] Matthew Kirschenbaum highlights this focus on materiality even more in his definition of DH, claiming that DH is "a scholarship and pedagogy that are bound up with infrastructure in ways that are deeper and more explicit than we are gen-

---

[16] Humanities scholars do not necessarily need to collaborate with data scientists directly. For example, humanities scholars might use libraries developed by those with expertise in data science (such as sklearn or keras). Direct collaboration is often better, however, given the need for humanities scholars to understand what particular algorithms are actually doing. In any case, the collaboration is real, and the DH project would fail without the help of data scientists.
[17] Timothy K. Beal, *The Rise and Fall of the Bible: The Unexpected History of an Accidental Book*, First Mariner books edition (Boston: Mariner Books, 2012), 78–79. See also Tibor Koltay, "Library and Information Science and the Digital Humanities," *Journal of Documentation* 72, no. 4 (July 2016): 781–92, https://doi.org/10.1108/JDOC-01-2016-0008.

erally accustomed to."[18] With the rise of computers for word processing and the internet for resource discovery and interaction, all humanities research is now digital to some degree. Yet, as Kirschenbaum's definition signals, DH work is purposefully self-conscious about both the material structures of data and the material media used for collection and dissemination of research findings.[19]

Libraries have to consider the distinct materialities of information in order to create appropriate environments for the preservation and circulation of resources in all of their various medial forms. In his careful analysis of the materiality of media archives in an increasingly digital infrastructure, Zach Lischer-Katz writes, "Librarians and archivists…are going to great lengths to produce effective policies and systems to organize and maintain the logical integrity of physical bits stored on magnetic discs and tapes, alongside their traditional custodianship of physical documents and artifacts."[20] Binding type, page material, ink composition, temperature, humidity, and lighting are examples of the materiality of information attended to in this traditional custodianship of codices mentioned by Lischer-Katz. With the rise of digital collections and the use of digital media, library attention to emerging materialities of information, such as bits, magnetic storage drives, and fiber networks, has only heightened. In fact, there is a growing movement among librarians to provide software archiving, which entails designing workflows and infrastructure to archive the whole system required to run an application.[21] This careful attention to the materialities involved in research and scholarship is shared by digital humanities approaches. In a DH project, a team has to consider things such as how their data will be structured, what visualization tools they will use to facilitate contact with the data, and what plat-

---

18 Matthew Kirschenbaum, "What Is Digital Humanities and What's It Doing in English Departments?" *ADE Bulletin* 150 (2010): 55–61, https://mkirschenbaum.files.wordpress.com/2011/03/ade-final.pdf. We find the use of "bound up" by Kirschenbaum here a bit humorous given the move away from the codex as dominant form for DH scholarship.
19 The Wikipedia definition of DH states this reflection on material medium explicitly. "Digital Humanities," *Wikipedia*, September 26, 2018, https://en.wikipedia.org/w/index.php?title=Digital_humanities&oldid=861261247.
20 Zach Lischer-Katz, "Studying the Materiality of Media Archives in the Age of Digitization: Forensics, Infrastructures and Ecologies." *First Monday* 22, no. 1 (2017). https://doi.org/10.5210/fm.v22i1.7263.
21 For examples of the significant thinking going toward software preservation, see "Preserving. Exe: Toward a National Strategy for Preserving Software." Accessed October 11, 2018. http://www.digitalpreservation.gov/meetings/preservingsoftware2013.html, Rios, Fernando. "The Pathways of Research Software Preservation: An Educational and Planning Resource for Service Development." *D-Lib Magazine* 22, no. 7/8 (July 2016). https://doi.org/10.1045/july2016-rios, and Kirschenbaum, Matthew. "Software, It's a Thing," July 25, 2014. https://medium.com/@mkirschenbaum/software-its-a-thing-a550448d0ed3.

forms they will use to host their data and their codebase for development, production, and archiving. Again, we see a shared set of capacities and dispositions among librarians and DH practitioners that suggest a productive collaborative relationship.

8 Getting People Involved

Our lab at Iliff started with a generic goal of learning about Natural Language Processing through building capacities in Python using the natural language toolkit. We quickly discovered two principles that encouraged involvement and adoption of these new methodologies. First, we try to take a project-based approach to our collaborative work as much as possible. There are times when we agree to learn a new technology together, just because we find it interesting. But, our most effective work together has been focused on a particular project that guides our learning and our development. For example, as part of a conference celebrating the legacy of our institution, we attempted to visualize the important foci and changes in conversation over the decades among our faculty. We used several decades of an internal periodical collection as our data set and used this project as a chance to learn more about Optical Character Recognition, preprocessing of text, topic modeling, word clouds, and text summarization using Google's PageRank algorithm. Having specific tasks we needed to accomplish and a deadline helped our team learn capacities that would be applied right away to a pressing problem to solve.

Collaborative public presentations can also be a great motivator to get the group working together toward something that can be shared with a broader public. Given the fundamental collaborative nature of DH work, these public fora can provide excellent opportunities for allowing additional voices into the design process to problematize assumptions and connect with other similar work going on in different contexts. Having targets for public demonstration of work in progress is a key strategy to interrupt the typical academic anxiety around sharing work before it is "finished."

The second principle that has helped encourage faculty participation and helped communicate the value of our work to the larger institution is what we call a translation-based approach to projects. As we mentioned above, one of the most exciting aspects of digital humanities scholarship is its ability to generate new questions and new approaches to problems that we have not imagined before. Yet, these new possibilities are inevitably connected to challenges and curiosities that have been around for a long time. A translational approach can be an effective way to get buy-in from administration and participation by resistant populations. We translate projects in two prominent vectors. We begin by listening to the questions and methodologies driving a faculty member's upcoming research project. Then our lab team translates aspects of this project into DH frameworks, connecting the already existing expertise, experience, and methodologies of the faculty member to ways in which DH could support, extend, and challenge their research through partnership with machines. For example, a faculty member at Iliff is working on the construction of gender, Judaism, and religion in the modern world by looking at three famous women who ran salons in Berlin at the start of the nineteenth century. Their correspondence was an extension of these intellectual and social gatherings (interestingly, one of them, Rahel Varnhagen, conceived of her correspondence as a collaborative and networked authorship, not unlike the model of project-based research we are pursuing in the Experimental Humanities Lab). Their novel use of language was an attempt to form religious and gendered identities not able to be accommodated by the extant German and Yiddish dialects. By creating machine readable versions of the critical editions of their correspondence, we can use machine learning tools to look for themes, patterns, and connections beyond what a human researcher might expect to find alone.

The second vector of translation is from the DH space into a vernacular that communicates to higher education administration and possible funding agencies. Here, we may begin with some interesting results we have found through machine assisted clustering or classification and translate both the methodology and the findings into language and frameworks that colleagues and administrators can digest and connect with. Often, this translation vector involves careful choices about data visualization, including clear and concise interpretations of the visualization to connect findings to strategic initiatives of the institution. This multi-vector translation approach to DH projects leverages the meaningful relationships between existing and emerging research methodologies in hopes of decreasing anxiety around newness, while increasing adoption and institutional buy-in.

9 Hybrid Approach

Our team in the EH Lab at Iliff has taken an intentional multi-layered hybrid approach to our work together. We combine regular synchronous and asynchronous interactions, with the synchronous being a hybrid of on-ground and online participation, involving staff, faculty, and students from different institutions in the process. We have found that a team messaging application can be an exceptional tool for facilitating ongoing conversations about specific coding challenges and theoretical topics that team members can participate in as they have availability.[22] These asynchronous discussion channels allow lab members to have focused conversation at the time of need and provide a searchable archive of resources and dialog we have shared with one another.

To facilitate our weekly hybrid synchronous gatherings, we have used a web conferencing tool to bring people together in a public space in our library. We have met in open, public space in the library on purpose, to promote and perform the kind of collaborative and experimental work we hope others will take up in our library. It has been critical that our library has sufficient WiFi infrastructure as well as easy to use audio and video capabilities to enable participants from Denver, Cleveland, Portland, and Chicago as well as many guests from other institutions such as Santa Clara University to join us for our weekly meetings. These hybridities can challenge the efficiency of the group due to the difficulties of asynchronous interaction, the technological complications of hybrid synchronicity, and the inevitable power dynamics involved in a hybrid community. Yet, we have seen the fruit of these complications in the constant emergence of difference that arises through the persistence and patience demanded by this hybrid approach.

10 Library Instruction

Many theological and religious studies libraries may find themselves on campuses that do not have digital humanities centers or experts available to lead the charge in these kinds of projects. However, insofar as digital methods can be considered a new and important form of information literacy, it makes sense that reference and instruction librarians will find themselves needing to be educators in this regard. Marissa Mouer has pointed out that subject librarians especially may find themselves teaching patrons (students and faculty) how to use digital tools for their research and scholarship.[23] Likewise, Janet Hauck outlines how librarians can use digital humanities projects as an opportunity to address many frames of the ACRL Framework for Information Literacy for Higher Education including "Information Creation as a Process," "Information has Value," "Authority Is Constructed and Contextual," and "Searching as Strategic Exploration."[24] In other words, digital humanities projects allow librarians to continue

---

22 Our team has chosen to use Slack available at https://www.slack.com/.
23 Mourer, "A Subject Librarian's Pedagogical Path in the Digital Humanities".
24 Janet Hauck, "From Service to Synergy: Embedding Librarians in a Digital Humanities Project"

what they have always done in terms of teaching information literacy; the only new piece is the proliferation of tools which are now available for the discovery, creation, and dissemination of information in the form of digital humanities projects.[25]

Digital humanities projects also provide another opportunity for librarians to provide embedded library instruction in the classroom.[26] In our context at Iliff we have found that some faculty have been open to having a librarian come to a classroom to teach students how to use a particular DH tool for a class project. For example, Voyant-tools is a widely used text-mining tool for visualizing textual data.[27] After introducing students to the basics of how to use a tool like Voyant, the librarian discussed with students how such visualizations are to be interpreted and used to support scholarly claims. The ability to effectively use and understand data visualization is a key component for information literacy today and digital humanities projects which require such information literacy provide opportunity for increased library instruction.

11 Scholarly Communications

One of the challenges of research and scholarship that embraces DH is folding the process and products from these emerging methodologies into the scholarly communications life-cycle so that scholars can get appropriate credit for this work in hiring, promotion, and tenure processes. DH projects are not easily reducible to print output in either monograph or article form, so often scholars participating in DH projects will have to do extra work to publish the research in a print form that can be vetted and evaluated by traditional mechanisms. Because libraries are embedded in the full scholarly communication lifecycle, they can be strong advocates for developing architecture to support access to and archival of DH scholarship as well as building capacities in students, faculty, and staff to participate in and evaluate DH work. Integrating DH projects into scholarly communication workflows will provide an increased incentive for scholars to learn these new skill sets and to participate in experimental projects. In turn, this will produce more people with the experience and skills to effectively

---

[25] For information on some of these tools from the perspective of theological librarianship see Kent T. K. Gerber, "DIKTUON: Getting Involved with the Digital Humanities in Theology, Biblical Studies, and Religious Studies," *Theological Librarianship* 9, no. 1 (January 2016): 5–10.
[26] Mourer, "A Subject Librarian's Pedagogical Path in the Digital Humanities."
[27] Stefan Sinclair and Geoffrey Rockwell, "Voyant Tools," accessed October 3, 2018, https://voyant-tools.org/.

evaluate DH projects in publication and promotion review processes. Finally, given its collaborative nature, a great deal of DH scholarship is done with a strong commitment to open access and open source movements. Libraries are well equipped to help scholars negotiate the complicated copyright issues related to use of data sets, making models available to different audiences, and maintaining scholarly identity. Promoting appropriate licensing on code repositories and embracing emerging mechanisms for tracking scholarly activity, such as ORCID iDs, are examples of ways libraries can support the collaborative and open approaches of DH, while protecting intellectual capital and scholarly identity.

The American Academy of Religion (AAR) established a task force to make recommendations to the religious studies guild (in the form of recommendations to the Board of the AAR) about the rapidly changing publishing environment. A significant part of the work of this task force was to develop a set of recommendations about how institutions can evaluate scholarship in digital humanities for hiring and promotion, and the responsibilities of researchers, deans, and personnel committees as the profession seeks to support this exciting and creative movement in the academic study of religion. The Experimental Humanities Lab at Iliff drafted the first version of these recommendations, and they were vetted and discussed at a session of THATCamp before the AAR Annual Meetings in November, 2016. They were adopted by the AAR Board of Directors in September 2018.[28]

12 Why Python?

One challenge that projects in the digital humanities have to address is the lack of coding experience among many humanities scholars.[29] When we began the Experimental Humanities Lab @ Iliff, we had one scholar with substantial coding experience and another scholar with substantial systems and database experience. The other scholars in our group had little to no experience in programming. We had to choose a programming language that people could learn quickly and that had excellent libraries that would support digital humanities work.

---

[28] See https://www.aarweb.org/AARMBR/About-AAR-/Board-of-Directors-/Board-Resolutions-/Guidelines-for-Evaluating-Digital-Scholarship.aspx.

[29] This trend is thankfully changing. Coding courses are now often a staple part of the curriculum in many undergraduate degree programs, and many newer humanities scholars are competent in coding.

We ended up choosing the Python programing language as our primary language for a number of reasons. First, and probably most importantly, our lab's lead data scientist had significant experience with Python. Second, we wanted the lab to be hands on with the materiality of code from the beginning, so we needed a shared learning task to get us past simply talking about doing things. Python provided a fairly low barrier to entry for getting our hands dirty. Third, many of those who began with the EH Lab were textualists, so it was natural for us to begin by exploring the possibilities for Natural Language Processing (NLP). The Python community had several important libraries (with good documentation) for getting started with NLP, which allowed us to explore high-level concepts without getting bogged down in the details.

As it turns out, the reasons Python constitutes a good choice for the collaborative and transdisciplinary work of the digital humanities extend far beyond those noted above. First, Python is notoriously readable, so that well-written Python code often reads almost like a sentence in English (or another natural language) might read. When humanists are working alongside mathematicians or data scientists, code readability matters. When just about anyone can read the code and understand its logic (at least, at the highest level), then the interface with the computer becomes transparent to all no matter what their discipline. Our library staff have taught informal classes on Python in our library to several interested people as a means to communicate both with the computer and with others doing work in the digital humanities.

Second, Python has many high-level, high-performance libraries that have garnered significant investment from the mathematics and scientific communities. Many of these libraries can be found in SciPy, "a Python-based ecosystem of open-source software for mathematics, science, and engineering."[30] SciPy includes NumPy (a library that performs high-level math and handles multidimensional arrays and matrices with ease),[31] the visualization library Matplotlib,[32] the data analysis package Pandas,[33] and the machine learning library scikit-learn.[34]

---

30 "SciPy.Org—SciPy.Org." Accessed October 11, 2018. https://www.scipy.org/. Much of SciPy depends upon code written in C or Fortran, which makes it fast when compared to native Python solutions.
31 "NumPy—NumPy." Accessed October 11, 2018. http://www.numpy.org/.
32 "Matplotlib: Python Plotting—Matplotlib 3.0.0 Documentation." Accessed October 11, 2018. https://matplotlib.org/.
33 "Python Data Analysis Library—Pandas: Python Data Analysis Library." Accessed October 11, 2018. https://pandas.pydata.org/.
34 "Scikit-Learn: Machine Learning in Python—Scikit-Learn 0.20.0 Documentation." Accessed October 11, 2018. http://scikit-learn.org/stable/.

For more advanced work in the digital humanities, Python can tap into the machine learning framework Tensorflow (originally developed by the Google Brain team) or the high-level API Keras that can run on top of Tensorflow.[35] These libraries provide state-of-the-art performance for many of the models used in the digital humanities.[36] The high-level nature of these libraries allows experts and novices in the sciences or mathematics to work side by side with humanities scholars who may be less savvy with these disciplines. Anyone who walks into our library can access these high-level libraries with a little instruction and explanation.

Third, Python is a great programming language to use in teaching. Its readability and numerous libraries allow students to do complex tasks in just a few concise, understandable lines. Since the field of digital humanities is relatively young, many who enter its ranks are relatively new to programming. Python makes an excellent choice of programming language to teach to newcomers. We have held introduction to Python classes in our library for both digital humanists and interested higher education staff, and almost everyone has profited from these classes despite their background.

Fourth, Python has excellent web frameworks that digital humanists can use to publish their results or learning. Libraries, as repositories of all kinds of learning, can offer demonstrations of conversations with computers or even runnable code in Jupyter notebooks as a kind of material artifact that embodies probabilistic production. Though one can focus on making reproducible models, one can also focus on creating models that contribute to probabilistic readings that extend beyond the probability based upon a reader's immediate or material circumstances.

Finally, Python is a widely popular programming language and thus continues to gain more traction in the digital humanities and in data science. This popularity was really pronounced in 2018 online surveys, where Python topped the lists for most popular programming languages.[37] The growing popularity of Python has led to an explosion of libraries and tools.[38] The official documentation is thorough and readable, and the official Python tutorial is a starting point for

---

35 "TensorFlow." TensorFlow. Accessed October 11, 2018. https://www.tensorflow.org/. For Keras, see "Keras Documentation." Accessed October 11, 2018. https://keras.io/.
36 We do not mean to imply here that Python is the only programming language that can provide state-of-the-art performance on these models.
37 "2018 Developer Skills Report by HackerRank." Accessed October 11, 2018. https://research.hackerrank.com/developer-skills/2018/.
38 148,000 as of August 11, 2018. https://pypi.org/.

learning the language. There are also vibrant online forums and chat rooms that provide a good place to ask questions and find answers to difficulties.

13 Challenges

There are both cultural and technological challenges that emerge in these kinds of experimental endeavors. The most persistent challenge for our lab has been sustaining sufficient institutional incentive for participants to invest in developing capacities and running experiments in DH. It takes a consistent time investment to become conversant in basic programming and to experiment with different DH research tools. With all of the other teaching, publishing, and administrative tasks demanded of faculty and staff, it is difficult for many to carve out consistent time to develop these new skills or even to become familiar with the literature in digital humanities. Taking a project-based approach to developing DH capacities has helped to focus our work on things that will have an immediate impact on someone's research, which can maintain some incentive for investment. Our lab's work on the AAR guidelines for evaluating digital scholarship is directly related to this incentive challenge. If we can encourage the dissertation, promotion, and tenure processes to embrace DH work as legitimate scholarship, then scholars will have a direct professional incentive for investing in the development of DH capacities.

One other consistent challenge our lab faces is supporting the different technological capacities and aptitudes among lab participants. The collaborative and interdisciplinary nature of DH work brings together people with very different levels of exposure to and comfort with digital technologies. This diversity of perspective and experience is a strength of DH, yet it can pose some challenges when trying to learn new methodologies or write code together. The challenge here is to create a lab environment that supports the different developmental levels, while pushing projects forward into new frontiers. On the technical side of this challenge, we have begun to use cloud-hosted Python notebook tools such as Google Colaboratory and Azure Notebooks. These hosted notebook environments allow us to learn, write, and share code and visualizations without having to maintain disparate integrated development environments on local machines. On the pedagogical side of this challenge, we are experimenting with moving to a research colloquium-based approach that emulates how many science labs work in research universities. Small teams will work together as needed on specific and focused projects at a pace that fits those participants. Regularly, we will gather as a large lab team and one group will be responsible for sharing their progress, challenges, and new tools they are exploring. Hopefully, this model will create an environment where many participants can experiment at their own pace, while still learning from the work of others in the lab.

14 Summary

Using our experiences from the Experimental Humanities Lab at the Iliff School of Theology, we have suggested that libraries focused on the study of theology and religion are excellent interfaces for the exploration of scholarship and pedagogy in digital humanities. These libraries and DH share a deep commitment to the values of collaboration, interdisciplinarity, and attention to medium. Taking a hybrid translational approach to DH projects can enhance the diversity of participants and encourage institutional buy-in. In the future, we are hoping to extend this hybrid translational approach by partnering with other religious and theological libraries to share resources and support the ongoing development of these spaces in several contexts. If you are interested in partnering, please contact us at the Experimental Humanities Lab at Iliff.[39]

---

[39] "Experimental Humanities." Iliff School of Theology. Accessed October 11, 2018. https://www.iliff.edu/experimental-humanities/.

Index

Abelson, Hal   134
Adams, Richard Manly, Jr.   3, 8
Adorno, Theodor   31, 34, 55
Al-Farabi, Abu Nasr   2
Anderson, Clifford B.   54, 84, 96, 97, 124, 127–129, 132, 136, 138–140, 142–143
Appleton, Nathaniel   20, 21
Asad, Talal   149
Augustine of Hippo   2
Austen, Jane   14, 16

Baskauf, Steve   6, 84, 86–88, 90
Batnitzky, Leora   38
Beal, Timothy   149
Bellamy, Joseph   20
Ben-Chorin, Schalom   47
Benda, Yuh-Fen   86
Berlin, Isaiah   1
Birnbaum, David J.   126, 128
Biswas, Gautam   139
Bloch, Ernst   50
Bonds, Leigh   2
Boss, Rob   19
Bourdieu, Pierre   149
Boyles, Christina   2
Brady, Corey   129, 139
Broll, Brian   129, 132, 139, 143
Buber, Martin   50
Bultmann, Rudolf   115
Burdick, Anne   151
Burrows, John F.   14, 16

Calico, Joy   128, 138, 143
Choiński, Michał   4
Cole, Katharine   126
Colman, Benjamin   20
Comte, Auguste   33
Cooksey, Mary Angelec   144
Croxall, Brian   112
Cukier, Kenneth   54

Dickinson, Jonathan   20-21
Dinkins, Stephanie   135

Dixon, Calvin P.   118
Drucker, Johanna   34, 41, 149-150
Du Bois, William Edward Burghardt   118
Durkheim, Emil   149

Eder, Maciej   18, 26
Edwards, Jonathan   4, 13, 15, 19–29
Ehrenberg, Hans   39
Ehrenberg, Rudolf   39
Erwig, Martin   134
Evans, Claire   135

Foucault, Michel   149
Foxcroft, Thomas   13–14, 23, 26–29
Fyfe, Paul   113

Garcia, Dan   130-131
Geertz, Clifford   149
Gil, Alex   2
Guelzo, Allen   19
Guzdial, Mark   125, 127

Habermas, Jürgen   31
Haden, Patricia   133
Hall, Wendy   135
Handelman, Matthew   4–5
Hartsell-Gundy, Arianne   147
Harvey, Brian   131, 134
Hauk, Janet   158
Hegel, Georg Wilhelm Friedrich   36-37
Heidegger, Martin   116
Hemings, James   34-35
Hensley, Merinda   8, 114-115
Hillmann, Diane   96
Hölderlin, Friedrich   43
Holmes, Sherlock   135
Hopper, Grace   135
Horkheimer, Max   31, 34, 55
Hudson, Scott E.   140
Hume, David   149

James, Henry   15
Jefferson, Thomas   35

Jockers, Matthew 15
Johnson, Julie 129

Kaehler, Siegfried A. 46
Kant, Immanuel 41, 149
Kellogg, John Harvey 61, 69
Kimnach, Wilson 26
Kirschenbaum, Matthew 154
Klein, Lauren 34, 44
Ko, Amy J. 135
Kracauer, Siegfried 39, 42, 47, 49-50
Kretzschmar, William A. 147

Langmead, Alison 126, 128
Ledeczi, Akos 129, 132
Ledeen, Ken 134
Lee, Harper 15
Lewis, Harry R. 134
Lischer-Katz, Zach 155
Liu, Alan 34
Lovelace, Ada 135

Mach, Ernst 33
Maimonides 2
Marcuse, Herbert 31, 35, 44, 53
Mayer-Schönberger, Viktor 54
McLuhan, Marshall 1
Michelson, David A. 6, 88-89, 127-128, 138
Miller, Tracy 6
Miller, William 58
Minkema, Kenneth 26
Mitchell, Susan 126
Modrow, Eckart 134
Mönig, Jens 131
Morozov, Evgeny 8
Mosteller, Frederick 14
Mouer, Marissa 158
Myers, Brad 140

Narasimham, Gayatrhi 3, 9, 124, 129, 136, 138-139
Nowviskie, Bethany 125

Papert, Seymour 140
Parsons, Dale 133
Parsons, Jonathan 20-21
Paulien, Jon 65

Pausch, Randy 140
Posner, Miriam 51
Potter, Harry 135
Potter, William Gray 147
Prince, Thomas 20-21

Ramey, Lynn 140
Resnick, Mitch 132, 142
Risam, Roopika 51
Rosenstock, Eugen 47
Rosenstock, Margrit 47
Rosenzweig, Adele 39
Rosenzweig, Edith 39
Rosenzweig, Franz 4, 32, 34–39, 41–44, 46–51, 53-54
Rosenzweig, Georg 39
Russell, John 8, 114-115
Rybicki, Jan 4, 29

Salesky, Winona 89
Schleiermacher, Friedrich 148
Schmidt, Benjamin 62
Schmidt, Doug 129
Schoenfield, Mark 139
Schwartz, Christine 3, 6-7
Sealy, William 86
Seltzer, Wendy 134
Sewall, Samuel 20
Simon, Ernst 39
Stiles, Ezra 20-21
Stoddard, Solomon 20-21, 27-28
Stommel, Jesse 114
Stout, Harry 18
Susman, Margarete 5, 39, 50-51
Sweeney, Douglas A. 20

Taylor, Michelle 128
Tennent, Gilbert 19-20
Thornton, Jacob 84
Thuesen, Peter J. 26
Thurman, Howard 120
Torrance, Iain 95-96, 100
Tramer, Hans 47
Turing, Alan 9, 48, 135-136
Turnbull, Ralph G. 22

Underwood, Ted 32

Varner, Stewart   113
Varnhagen, Rahel   157

Wallace, David L.   14
Walmsley, Priscilla   97
Walton, Jonathan   118
Weber, Max   149
Weintrop, David   141–142
Wernke, Steve   89

Wheelock, Eleazar   20-21
White, Ellen G.   58, 60
White, James   60
Whitefield, George   19–22
Wieringa, Jeri E.   5
Wilensky, Uri   141

Yeager, Jonathan M.   26-27

www.ingramcontent.com/pod-product-compliance
Lightning Source LLC
Chambersburg PA
CBHW070555240426
43664CB00050B/2696